TELESALES SECRETS

A GUIDE TO SELLING ON THE PHONE

Monaco 2014

©Acanexus, Monaco 2014

ISBN 978-82-92944-12-7

First Edition: January 2014
Author: Claes Simonsen
Production: Acanexus Publishing
Cover: Jana Rade, impact studios

ACKNOWLEDGMENTS

This book could not possibly have come about without the interesting, exciting and challenging discussions I have had with the many sellers and sales managers I have worked with. I particularly want to thank Viktor Stromberg and Robin Axelsson, together with whom many of the theoretical ideas in this book have been formed, and Sebastian Scherman, Niclas Ryegard, Jane Rohdin and Roy Olsson whom I have known for a long time and who are probably some of the best sellers I have ever worked with.

PREFACE

Good sellers tend to be considered important people in their businesses, at least for purely financial reasons, so it can come as no surprise that quite a lot of sellers move from sales into management. As a serial entrepreneur, I took the other direction and moved from management into sales (sometimes things really get done well only if you do it yourself). This has probably given me a very different approach to selling and sales technique. Most managers seem to think that their influence over sales results is limited to *thinking* "Why the hell aren't you guys selling more?" (passive sales management) or *screaming* "Why the hell aren't you guys selling more?" (active sales management).

When screaming didn't work anymore, I realized the only way to really influence sales results from a management position was to develop proper sales techniques, tools and training. These circumstances have given me a very theoretical approach to selling; my aim has been to understand logically and empirically what leads to sales. This contrasts with the approach of those who perhaps started selling well themselves and then tried to understand what they were doing well and writing it down in a book. This is particularly true for what I very derogatively and quite unfairly refer to as the "happy-clappy school of sales technique." Someone blessed by nature or fortune with good sales skills will naturally soon realize that he sells well on days when he is happy, positive and "pumped." In my opinion this has led to many sales books overemphasizing "positive thinking."

Positive thinking, although a very nice attitude to life, is not a sales technique. If you're a terrible seller and you remain positive over time, you're probably also an idiot. Positive thinking is as helpful to a seller as it is to a brain surgeon: nice to see, but no substitute for years of medical theory and training. If I had to choose between a positive surgeon with no medical training and a depressed surgeon with years of training and experience, I'd prefer to hand the knife to the latter. Of course, and this is where my criticism becomes a bit unfair, what you really want is a well-trained surgeon who feels pretty confident he's not going to kill you. In sales, what you want is a well-trained seller who understands all the sales theory and has good, fundamental sales skills to fall back on. And then you also want him to be happy and self-confident. This book is basically about the technical skills of selling. But there is a little happy-clappy bit at the end too, just for that extra oomph.

You might think, from the examples in this book, that I have spent my life selling printers and photocopiers. I haven't. In fact I have never tried to sell a printer in my life, except when—at the age of 12—I tried to convince my mother that she really had to buy my nine-pin printer because I was desperate to buy a new laser printer. It was probably about that time I learned that the arguments you have for selling something and the argument you give to the customer for buying that something, do not have to be the same.

In this book, however, I have stuck to examples relating to printers and photocopiers for one simple reason: When you sell life insurance, trademark registrations, credit default swaps and most other products out there, a million different product-related questions come with the product and may come up during a call. Although obviously very important to the sales process for each product, the actual answers to such questions don't belong in a book about sales technique. Printers are fairly simple, though. They are either color or black and white, and they print X amount of sheets per hour. That makes the examples in this book easier to read and understand from a sales technique perspective. If you happen to sell printers, you are, of course, in luck.

In this book I have marked off sections of particular interest with icons in the margins: "smart tip," "remember" and "warning." This layout has been popularized by the "For Dummies" books, presumably to make the books look longer. I find the style useful both because it facilitates quick browsing and because it leaves plenty of space for your own comments.

On a flowchart of the sales process, most commonly a "lead" is someone who might be worth contacting; then following a successful sale, the lead will become a "customer." Curiously "lead" in this sense does not appear in most dictionaries, although it is obviously closely related to the definition of lead as "a suggestion or piece of information that helps to direct or guide" (Think "clue"). In the sales industry, however, the use of "lead" referring to a person to whom you can potentially sell, a "potential future customer," is fairly well-established. The word "prospect" is also used, and what is defined as a lead or a prospect varies greatly from company to company, though in my experience "prospect" is most commonly used to refer to leads who have taken some active steps to indicate interest (clicking on emails, ordering information and so on).

In this book, mainly just to get the text to flow a bit better, I have used the words "lead," "customer" and "potential customer" interchangeably. They all indicate someone you are trying to sell to.

CONTENTS

"I thought you said your mother was home."
"She is, but this isn't where I live."

INTRODUCTION

A SHORT HISTORY OF SELLING

"(...) Up to this time, you have carefully abstained from pressing your customer to buy. Your whole effort has been directed to the one prime object of creating desire. But now comes the supreme moment. 'Subscribe' is an odious word to many persons. Therefore, never use it. Instead of asking, 'Will you subscribe,' say, 'your name will be in good company, you see. It comes next after your neighbor, Mr. So-and-So,' or, 'on the next page after Squire So-and-So,' or something of this sort. With this, place the prospectus or order-book squarely before him.

Bates Harrington wrote these words in 1879 in a book with a lengthy, but very honest title, "How 'Tis Done – A Thorough Ventilation of the Numerous Schemes Conducted by Wandering Canvassers, or Advertising Dodges for the Swindling of the Public." It's often referred to as the first proper sales manual. As the title may indicate it was not intended as such—on the contrary it was intended as a warning and a teaching tool for the public on how to avoid being taken in by pushy salespeople. As is often the case with such warnings, particularly when they take the shape of a 336-page book, it wasn't read by those who wanted to avoid being taken in by scammers, but rather extensively studied by those who wanted either to learn how to scam or, more innocently, those who wanted to learn how to sell quickly. In any case it was far from the first sales manual; in reality there were a number of books published at about the same time giving extensive advice on sales techniques—advice of which the basics remain the same to this day. This was a period of rapid change; products were getting more complicated, consumers more demanding and businesses were expanding their markets geographically. Yelling "Cheap tomatoes, cheap tomatoes. Get them here" may be good enough for a market vendor, but it won't sell many insurance policies or much advertising space. The modern, active selling was a result of changing times; good products suddenly were no guarantee for success. You also had to get your offers out to the consumers in a manner that consumers could understand and that was more efficient than your competitors'.

And so, gradually a class of truly professional sellers emerged. Those companies that understood how to use the newly developed active sales technique to their advantage could, like today, corner markets and make enormous profits. Possibly the first to understand this on a truly professional basis was John Henry Patterson. In 1884 he bought the patents for Ritty's Incorruptible Cashier and formed National Cash Register Inc., NCR for short. Ritty had managed to sell only about a dozen of his cash registers. But Patterson created a sales force working purely on commission, simply called the American Selling Force, and gave them extensive training and, possibly for the first time in history, a standard sales script to follow.

As such, Patterson's system can possibly be said to be the grandfather of all modern call centers. Granted he used no phones, but the structure of training and its modus operandi have been a model for efficient sales structures for over one hundred years. His methods were highly successful—and in fact NCR survives to this date.

On a side note, Patterson also became famous for firing Thomas Watson, who would later go on to become the General Manager and President of CTR (today known as IBM). In fact, so many prominent businessmen were trained—and dismissed—by Patterson that work experience from NCR at the time was de facto considered the equivalent of an MBA degree.

Since this is the introductory chapter, I'll indulge myself and include a few phrases from Patterson's training manual. Remember that we're still in the 1880s:

After you have made your proposition clear and you feel sure that the merchant realizes the value of the cash register, do not ask for an order, take for granted that he will buy. Say to him "Mr. Smith, what color shall I make it?" or "How soon do you want delivery?" ...

Take out your order form, fill it out, and handing him your pen say, "Just sign where I have made the cross."

If he objects, find out why, answer his objections and again prepare him for signature. Make the merchant feel that he is buying because of his own good judgment ... find out the real reason why he is hesitating and chances are that that is the very reason why he should buy. Concentrate your whole force on one good strong point, appeal to judgment, get him to acknowledge that what you say is true, then hand the pen to him in a matter-of-fact way and keep on with what you were saying. This makes signing the logical and obvious thing to do.

Many modern sales books are in fact little but lengthy rewrites of Patterson's sales manual. The advice it offered was clearly revolutionary at the time. Just a few decades earlier asking "so, you want it or not?" was considered sufficient sales technique, and here this manual in detail describes how to conduct a lengthy conversation, analyze customer needs and efficiently and elegantly close the sale there and then. But although many of the techniques are still of value, the fact is that the world has changed since 1884. Products are even more complicated, customers are more used to smart sales people and consumer protection laws with cooling off periods mean that a signature may not be enough if the customer changes his mind when you walk out the door.

In fact the whole buying process has changed. Just in the past few decades, the workload of decision-makers has increased dramatically. A few decades ago hardly anyone had heard of email, no one was spending four hours a day going through his or her inbox and then another few hours a day surfing online, constantly being bombarded with smart targeted ads.

Gatekeepers, such as secretaries screening letters and phone calls, have been replaced by laptops, mobile phones and automated switchboards. As a result, today's decision-makers are bombarded with both internal and external communication. If you add up all emails, phone calls, voice messages, Internet ads, TV- and radio ads, letters and faxes, the average decision-maker is receiving thousands of offers a day. The world is clearly more confusing than in 1884. It takes much more to get your message through.

And perhaps most importantly, today a large portion of sales are not completed face to face. No use pushing your order book over the desk if the customer is actually on the phone.

WHY SELLING ON THE PHONE IS DIFFERENT

When I ask new sellers why they think selling on the phone is different from other types of sales, the most common answer is probably some sort of variation on "because the customer isn't physically in the same room as you." They are of course absolutely right. And if they were competing on a game show with "extremely obvious" as the topic, they would certainly do well. But it doesn't really do us much good when trying to adapt our sales technique. So let us try to analyze the differences a bit deeper.

On the phone a seller loses many of his traditional strengths. You can look as honest as you want, you can control your body language perfectly, you can lean forward at all the right times but it won't do you an ounce of good. All the client can hear is the sound of your voice. Like a comedian used to doing live shows suddenly getting a radio gig, the seller may think that words are his tool, but put him on a phone and he soon realizes that he is used to supplementing his words with a lot of small extra actions. Take away those extra actions and suddenly closing a deal becomes much, much harder. Working on the phone requires better understanding of sales techniques, a better control of the conversation than any other type of sales.

Another interesting fact about selling on the phone is that clients seem to become smarter. I know it sounds odd, but research show that it is much harder to detect a lie when you are talking face to face than on the phone. In fact, while most people will score no better than a random flip of the coin when detecting a lie in a physical meeting, a 1994 British study showed that participants who only listened, without visual cues, achieved an impressive 73% accuracy rate in detection of lies and truths. Add to this the fact that people in general are more suspicious when approached by a seller on the phone than a seller they meet face to face, and it becomes obvious that selling on the phone is hard work and requires sharper technical skills than perhaps any other type of selling.

In addition, while most people would be reluctant to physically carry you out of their meeting room, a customer on the phone can make you go away by a simple click of a button. On the phone, by default the client is in charge. So on the phone a seller must be aggressive in his tactics, yet appear not to be pushy at all.

There are of course a number of positive sides to selling on the phone. Speed is probably the biggest single advantage. In seconds you can reach potential customers who would otherwise take you hours to meet in person; from the phone the entire world can be your market. This not only reduces the costs per lead contacted, but also hugely increases time efficiency. The number of calls per day of course varies greatly. While a sales agent in a cold calling call center with a predictive dialer can dial 400 to 500 numbers in a day, a senior in-house sales representative may call only 5, 10 or 20 leads in a day. But in both cases speed, efficiency and cost remain the main advantages of phone sales.

These advantages apply to the potential customer too. Not only does he save time by not having physical meetings, but through the phone he can reach multiple potential suppliers and achieve better deals than he could otherwise expect. Cold calling has achieved a bit of a bad reputation, yet it does offer great advantages to the customers. Smaller companies that could not otherwise afford to get their message out to the customers through traditional advertising channels can get their offers through to a large number of customers, to the mutual benefit of both parties.

Let's be honest: the industry most threatened by cold calling is the media. If a business owner is prevented from contacting the potential customers directly, either through direct mailings, emails or phone calls, the media will eventually achieve a total monopoly on the communication between businesses and their customers. Newspapers and television stations would obviously greatly prefer to be the only means of reaching new clients. No wonder then that the same media is only too happy to present cold calling in a bad light. Let's face it: How much trouble is it really receiving an email you didn't ask for or a call from someone asking you if you might be interested in their products, considering the fact that most people have no problem accepting that their favorite sports programs and TV series are being interrupted every 10 or 15 minutes with five-minute long sales messages? Is it really the consumers complaining or have we just allowed ourselves to be told by the media that cold calling is bad, and accepted the argument without much logical thought? In my opinion, direct marketing—be it mail, emails, faxes or cold calling—are vital in order to make sure new startups can compete with the big brands. If TV, radio and newspaper were the only channels available to new companies, the consumers would be the biggest losers.

One unique aspect of phone selling is the cold call. Though cold calling is far from the only way of selling on the phone (in fact, many sales centers do not cold call at all), it is perhaps what most people associate with phone sellers. For both the seller and the customer it is a curse and a blessing. For the customer it can mean wasted time, but also access to bigger discounts and products from companies that could not afford to reach him through traditional marketing means. For the seller it offers unique opportunities and a "kick" that few other ways of selling can provide, buy also hours of disappointment and frustration.

Cold calling today remains vastly different from new sales and marketing techniques such as mass emailing, mass faxing, mass voice messaging and similar methods in the sense that while all these are passive techniques, cold calling is active. A good seller, therefore, can achieve fantastic results based on the sheer volume of calls he can make. And while cold calling may seem monotonous, the satisfaction of calling a random person, explaining the product and closing a sale—there and then in the first call—can perhaps not be rivaled by any other type of sale.

In fact, I recently met a seller who used to work for me doing cold calling many years ago, while he was in his early twenties. He now works as a sales manager for a large technology company, closing deals worth possibly millions of dollars. Yet he told me that the sense of achievement of closing these big deals, after weeks and weeks of negotiations, come nowhere close to the achievement he felt when closing 10 or 15 small deals in a day on the phone from cold calling.

In this book we will look at all the aspects of successful phone selling, from the preparations before a successful call to the closing of a deal. Because phone selling requires better control of the sales conversation than most other types of sales, for the above mentioned reasons, a substantial part of the book is spent on looking at ways of staying in charge of the call—guiding the client toward a close without seeming pushy. I will show you a number of techniques you can use to keep control of the conversation and how you can guide a client back to your own pitch if the call starts going off track.

Though cold calling is only a small part of the art of selling on the phone, the special skills and techniques it requires mean that I, throughout the book, have given some special attention to it. Most of the focus obviously centers on the opening of calls. The skills required to get your foot in the door on a pure cold call may be unique, but it is nevertheless something that can be learned technically. These are also skills that can come in handy even if you are mainly contacting warm leads and may help any seller to develop good sales techniques.

I have also dedicated quite a bit of space to objection handling. This is probably the aspect of a sales call that most separate a good seller from the sales geniuses. A sales genius knows how to use objections from the customer to drive the call forward and to close. The best sellers love objections because they can use those very objections to close the deal.

I have also included a section on how to successfully handle gatekeepers. Gatekeepers, such as switchboard operators, secretaries and PAs may be encountered in any type of sale, but they are probably more common when selling on the phone. Without proper skills to handle the gatekeeper, you may never even get a chance to do your sales pitch at all.

Finally I have dedicated a short section of the book to new technologies, such as SMS, voice mail messages and similar.

These tools are more and more frequently used by phone sellers to reach leads—and if handled correctly they can improve sales. If handled badly they can, however, have the opposite effect.

"Daddy must work because he can't finish it all in the office."
"Why don't they just put him in a slower group?"

PREPARATIONS

PREPARE TO SELL

Two chapters that can usually safely be skipped in books about selling are the chapters on motivation and the chapters on preparation. These are usually collections of obvious and patronizing blah-blah. Their main purpose can only be presumed to be to fill up pages that would otherwise look embarrassing blank. The phrase "failing to prepare is preparing to fail" seems to be mandatory. I will try to be somewhat less obvious by looking a little deeper into why we prepare.

We clearly prepare to improve our performance. Like a professional football player practices and prepares to improve his skills, the professional seller prepares to improve the quality of his sales calls. But in phone selling, preparation needs to go farther than that. As I have mentioned earlier, two of the biggest advantages of selling on the phone are efficiency and speed. And good preparations, such as call lists, a well-prepared sales script and so on are needed to maximize this advantage.

In addition, the professional phone seller needs to prepare to keep motivation high. As with any type of sales, motivation is a key factor to success. But in phone selling, lack of preparation can lead to monotony and boredom and in the end significantly impact your motivation and performance.

Let's start by looking at preparation for efficiency. If you're on an autodialer managed by someone else, you're in luck. Most of this will be taken care of for you. If you are not on an autodialer, though, you need to make sure that you plan your day properly.

When you call manually, you should always call from a list. Do not make one call and then start looking for another lead to call. Put together lists of leads to call and then call them. Phone selling is about efficiency and pace. You need a high pace and a good rhythm in order to make sales on the phone. You can never achieve this by calling one lead, then spend another 3, 5 or 15 minutes looking for the next person to call. Use a spreadsheet and plan a whole session of calling. This can be all the calls for that day or all the calls before lunch. Just make sure your list is long enough that you can keep at it for enough time to "get in the zone."

> *"The zone" or "the flow" is a mental state often associated with sports, but equally relevant to any type of activity requiring a significant amount of focus and attention. Researchers generally postulate two conditions required to get into "the zone": the activity you are performing has clearly defined goals and the feedback is immediate. This obviously matches pretty much the condition for phone sales. It is easy to define a clear goal (whether it is closing a contract or booking a meeting) and you will know immediately whether you succeeded or not. A successful phone seller will use this to force himself into a flow of work where he forgets time and space and focuses only on the conversations and the results.*

When you are trying to sell, the world around you should fade into the background. If your focus is not 100% on your pitch, you will never be successful as a seller.

Another reason we want to make sure we have long lists of leads to call is that, at least on bad days, phone selling can be mentally very hard. If you have a break between each call, your brain will try to make that break last as long as possible.

While looking in the Yellow Pages for a lead to call, you suddenly realize that a cup of coffee might be a good idea. And then a short bathroom break. And then you just need to check your email to see if that lead from yesterday has answered back. And suddenly the whole day has passed and you have done nothing. The whole point of phone selling, the main advantages it has over all other types of sales, are efficiency and speed. If you can't remain efficient, if you can't keep the speed up, you will never succeed. So make sure you put together a good list of leads to call. Long enough to make sure you get into your stride and focus on nothing but your sales pitch.

Talking about call lists, try to prevent starting your day or phone session by putting the list together. Instead put the list together before you leave the workplace the day before. Getting off to an efficient start is extremely important, and sitting down to do administrative work first thing in the office is not the right way to start the day. Toward the end of the day, you will in any case start to tire. You will be less focused and less efficient on the phone. It's a perfect time to stop selling and start preparing for the next day to be successful.

In my experience the two most critical periods of time during the working day are the morning and just after lunch. Both require an extra mental effort to force yourself into the right flow. If you fail to do so, you will soon realize you have wasted the entire day.

When you are putting together call lists, make sure that you have all the information there that you need for the call and that the information is easy to read. Write clearly if you do this by hand or use large font if you do this on a computer. There is nothing more painful for a sales professional to hear than a junior seller starting off a call with "Hi, is this Mr., eh, um, eh, Mr. Roo, no, Mr. Brooks?" I have even heard call center staff being moved from one project to another, not knowing on behalf of which company they were calling.

Although it is easy to understand how this can happen, it is not easy to forgive. Starting a call with "Have you considered pet insurance for your dog?" only to be told the lead doesn't have a dog is not a good start if you're actually trying to sell timeshare. Just as it is easy to understand how a golf pro might be overcome by nerves on the first tee and hit a ball straight into the crowd, it is easy to understand how a seller moved from one project to another might get confused. But in the end, just as it is the golf pro's job not to be overcome by nerves, so it is the phone seller's job not to get his products mixed up.

If you don't know who you are calling or what you are selling, how can you possibly expect to sell? I know it is human to err, but there are limits. A seller not knowing who he is calling or what he is selling is like a hockey player walking on to the ice only to realize he has forgotten his skates.

Preparing for efficiency ties neatly into preparing for higher motivation. Nothing can be more demoralizing than spending an hour on the phone without getting through to someone you can pitch properly.

The first call of the day ideally happens within 30 seconds of sitting down at your desk. No coffee, no chat, no checking email. Just straight on the phone. Simply write a name and a phone number on a Post-it note and stick it on your screen or phone before you leave in the evening and pick up the note and make the call as soon as you walk in. Some sales books suggest making the first call of the day an easy call, such as a thank-you call to someone who bought yesterday or a call to the nice, but hopeless lead who definitively wants this "but just needs to talk to his wife/brother/accountant first." Any positive call, where you have little to lose, just to get you going. The idea is that you get yourself going well with a low threshold.

I like the idea, but find that it really works the best in sales organizations with low sales volumes—where it is accepted not to have a few sales before lunch. If you work with a type of product or service where your target is 3, 5 or 10 sales per day, I personally prefer to get my sellers started selling right off the bat. If you are under a constant pressure to deliver sales volume, the first few hours seem to be when you mentally decide whether this is a good or bad day. If you have no sales after a few hours, by lunch and so on, panic has a tendency to set in, and the calls become more desperate and frustrated.

The most essential part of your preparation, though, is to prepare for a higher quality of selling. Before you lift up the phone you need to know exactly what you want to achieve and what you need to say in order to achieve it. This means writing a sales pitch script. I don't care how long you have been working in sales; you should always write down a sales script. Even if you get a script from the company your work with, you should write down your own version. Writing down the entire pitch yourself forces you to think through the various aspects of the call you are about to make. What are the selling points? What objections may the client have? How much information do you need to give and what techniques can you use to move from the information phase and on to the closing phase.

> *Some companies will object strongly to someone going off the predefined script. But even if you will never use the script you write, making your own script as a mental exercise is important. It acts like a simulator for your actual selling and gives you a chance to think through every phase of your pitch and identify risks and opportunities.*

The sales script should always have the aim of the call written in bold on top. Of course the ultimate goal in selling is closing the deal. But some calls are made with the aim of arranging a meeting; some calls are made to close immediately. Your pitch, your voice, your attitude throughout the call must be adapted to that aim. Every word in the pitch should be moving you closer to that goal. Sadly I see many sales scripts that seemed to be written with no particular goal in mind at all. Sometimes it seems that the person who wrote the script, whether a team leader or sales manager, or the seller himself, simply wrote down the words that came into his mind. And in the order he thought of them. That is bad. Not a single word should go into a sales script that hasn't been considered and reconsidered and found to be essential in order to move the call forward toward its ultimate goal. Let me exemplify. Here is a call script I came across online:

"Good afternoon, this is Steven Johnson with Magnetic IT. Have I caught you in the middle of something?"

(…)

"Let me just explain briefly why I'm calling. Magnetic IT is a small firm established in 1982 that focuses on helping our clients to make significant savings in their IT hardware by offering cheap software and hardware modifications that on average can prolong the lifespan of your IT equipment, such as PCs, scanners and printers by up to 30%!"

(…)

"Do you know your current spending on IT hardware?"

There is so much wrong with this script, it is hard not to be physically sick. But the main problem is that it just seems to be words with no aim in mind. The seller is talking simply to talk, not talking to sell. In what way will asking "Have I caught you in the middle of something?" move the call toward a sale? If you get a "no" here—and trust me 80% of the people you call will automatically say they are busy if you give them a chance, even if they are just sitting at their desk having a quiet cup of coffee—how will that have helped your chances of getting a sale? You will then have to explain that "this will only take a minute of your time" and you are now slightly farther away from closing a deal than you were before you picked up the phone in the first place. And why does the seller feel the need to tell the client that the company he is calling from is a small company or that it was formed in 1982? I am sure they are very proud of their long history, and being a well-established firm may be important to the final decision-making process of the customer. But not at this stage. The seller hasn't even said why he is calling!

A sales call will have several distinct phases. I will talk more about those later. For now it is sufficient to point out that when you work on your sales script, in addition to the overall goal of the call, you must keep in mind which phase you are in and what the aim of each phase is. For the opening phase, your goal is to make sure you get your foot through the door. In the information phase—or the "What I can do for you phase?" as I prefer to call it (see page 51), your aim is to arouse customer interest. Everything you say in this phase should work toward that aim, in addition to, of course, keeping the overall goal in mind. And when you get to the closing phase, it is all about taking the order down. This is why, as you will see in page 55, I do not allow sellers to revert back to product information in this phase; it simply doesn't help the closing. Keep all this in mind when writing your sales script.

> *The most important part of a sales script, though, is often not what is being said, but what is not being said. A good sales script makes the customer talk to you, while you at the same time remain in control of the call through questions and gentle prodding. Dialogues sell, monologues don't. If you prefer to talk rather than to listen, become a politician.*

There are some inherent dangers with using written sales scripts. The first is that sticking a sales script in front of an inexperienced seller sometimes results in the seller turning into some sort of unthinking robot. His voice will change from natural to unnatural, his pace and timing will change (usually he will talk faster and skip natural breaks) and he tends to stop listening to the customer entirely. For this reason some high profile sales coaches recommend never using a sales script. This is, of course, insanity; as far as I am concerned all those who have paid for advice like that should call and ask for their money back. Saying that we should dispense of sales scripts just because it makes some inexperienced sellers sound like idiots is no more intelligent than saying we should skip all scripts in movies because some bad actors sound like they are reading their lines from a piece of paper, and that from now on every movie will be based on only improvisation. Suggesting scrapping all sales scripts just because some sellers don't handle them well is like curing a headache by chopping your head off. The way to handle the difficulties some people experience when faced with a pre-written sales script is (just as in the acting business) practice, practice, practice. The sales script forms the foundation of what you will say on the phone, but it is not enough in itself. You must also practice the execution. This is done through role play and sound and video recording—and of course real phone selling experience. Practice the pace, practice your voice and practice your pauses. The aim is to turn your sales pitch into something that sounds like a natural conversation. Basically the good seller must learn how to be a good actor.

 As part of your preparation for your calls you should also set some clear targets for yourself. These targets should be written down on a piece of paper. Loose targets in your head simply don't have the same effect.

You should set goals not only for your sales. Sales targets are obviously important to track your performance, but on their own they don't help you identify where things may have gone wrong. So also make sure to set tactical targets like "I will make 120 calls today," "I will talk to 60 decision-makers," "I will make 20 full pitches" and so on. Set targets for every difficult phase in your sales pitch. If you are selling a product that requires immediate payment by a credit card on the phone, for example, number of credit cards asked for and number of credit cards actually taken down are obvious milestones for which you should have clear targets.

By setting several intermediate targets it suddenly becomes much easier to identify problems or phases of your sales pitch that can be improved. If you made the number of calls you targeted, but only spoke to 20% of the number of decision-makers you expected, maybe it's time to look at where you find your numbers and dialing lists. If, on the other hand, you reached the number of decision-makers expected, but you only moved on from the introduction phase in half the number of calls planned, then perhaps you should start rewriting your call opener.

The need to measure your results against your targets means that you must keep some sort of simple statistics throughout your working day. They don't have to be advanced or complicated. A piece of paper or a Post-it with a line or an "x" for each entry will usually be fine. The stats are there just for you to compare with your targets.

At the end of the working day, compare your statistical notes with your targets and try to find out if there are any parts of your sales process where you have underperformed. Before you leave for the day, write down a few things that you will try to do differently tomorrow. This way you will be able to walk into the office the next day, feeling confident that you will do even better. This process should be repeated every day, even if you are feeling on top of the world.

I always tell the sellers I coach to look at themselves as much as professionals as do top athletes. The elite of the sales world can often make as much as the best athletes (see page 177), although you may never have heard of them or seen them on television. But in order to reach that level you need to take your sales career very seriously indeed. You wouldn't expect to become a professional golfer or a top football player without endless hours of practice. So don't expect to become a top seller without a similar investment in time and effort either.

MANAGING YOUR TIME

When we think about time management, we think mostly about cutting down on time waste. And obviously that is an important part of improving efficiency. Let's face it; life today is full of time leeches. The average US adult today spends 25 minutes every day on Facebook and other social media, 250 minutes checking and replying to emails and 115 minutes surfing the web. Add those together and you get an astonishing 4.8 hours per day, spent on just those three activities! We haven't included time spent chatting with colleagues, making coffee, staring at the wall—or time spent looking for that piece of paper where you wrote down the phone number to that lead who definitely was going to buy today and so on and so forth. And yet, 4.8 hours per day amounts to an absurd 219 working days a year! Granted, not all those hours are wasted in the office—some are wasted at home too. But it gives you an idea what sort of potential for improved performance most people have. And perhaps also why some people who seem to have all the time in the world never get anything done, while other people, who seem extremely busy all the time, can still take on and handle it all. People who learn efficient time management are usually people who are successful, not just in their business lives but in their personal lives too.

There is a saying, sometimes attributed to Lucille Ball, that goes something like "If you want something done, ask a person who is already busy." Though it may initially seem counterintuitive, it is a rule I have followed throughout my professional career—and it has nearly always turned out to be true. People who have a lot to do usually get a lot done— or they wouldn't remain in their positions. People with all the time in the world seem to be overwhelmed by the simplest of tasks. Ask a lazy person to do nothing but checking that there is enough coffee and sugar in the office breakroom, and in six months he'll be asking for an assistant because he is overworked.

It is possible to learn efficient time management. In fact it isn't very hard at all. The general rule is "If it doesn't matter or if you can't influence it, don't bother with it." It's as simple as that. It should be pretty damn obvious, but I don't know how many times I have seen sellers spending half their day clicking "send and receive" in their email because they are waiting for an order confirmation from a lead who "definitely said he'd be sending it today." Clicking send and receive every five minutes is not going to make a difference. When he sends it, you'll know pretty soon anyway. In the meantime just go and sell to someone else.

Of course not all time spent off the phone is time wasted. Good time management is really about spending your time where it matters. What we really want to improve is the time-to-sale ratio. Not preparing properly—not knowing the lead's name or details—may cost you a few minutes here and there. But it is definitely not going to improve your time-to-sale ratio.

What you are looking for is the perfect balance between good preparation and enough phone time. And again we can fall back on our simple rule: if it doesn't matter, don't spend time on it. Ask yourself this question from time to time throughout the day. Or stick "Does it really matter?" on a note next to your keyboard. Here is the essence of a call I heard while walking through a sales room just a few days back:

SELLER: Hi! This is John from ABC Inc. Am I talking to Jane?
CUSTOMER: Yes. What is this about?

> *SELLER: I think we spoke back in February or March? I*
> *wanted to discuss your software licensing plan.*
> *CUSTOMER: I am certain we spoke, and as I told you*
> *back then I am not interested.*

This is bad time management. Perhaps John got a few calls more made that day, but by not taking the time to keep and check his notes, he was really wasting much more time than he was gaining. A good sales call is about offering the customer something of benefit to him. If you don't know if or when you've spoken to the client before, all you can do is your standard pitch which you most likely already tried without success. And the customer can be pretty sure the call is going to be a waste of time as soon as he realizes you don't even know if you have spoken to him before or not. What John should have done is to have spent 30 seconds making a short note from the first call, noting what they talked about, what the client's situation and objection was, and another 30 seconds before the next call to adapt his pitch to fit the situation. This call could have been completely different if it had started like this:

> *SELLER: Hi Jane! It's John from ABC Inc. We spoke in*
> *February about your software licensing plan. How*
> *have you been?*
> *CUSTOMER: Um, good. Was this the offer for discounted*
> *Office licenses?*
> *SELLER: Sure was! Last time you said that you already*
> *had a license plan with your current supplier, but that*
> *it was expiring in June. Now, I have some notes from*
> *last time, and I can see that you were paying $ 107 per*
> *user with your current supplier. I promised to talk to*
> *my manager to see if we could beat that price, and I*
> *have been allowed to offer you this at $ 105. You said*
> *you had 250 users, right?*

Getting a call off to a start like this is time well spent. That is efficient time management and definitely worth the investment of a few seconds to make proper notes after a call.

Many sellers on commission don't fully understand how much impact just a small increase in efficiency can have on their income. Let's say you work eight hours per day and three of those hours are spent on administrative tasks (filling in sales forms, handling existing customers and so on).

> *Three hours may sound a lot, but in my experience a seller will easily spend 20 minutes from the time she closes one sale until she is on the phone pitching again. After a few high fives, sales forms, email confirmation to the client, a celebration coffee and a quick cigarette and you can easily double that amount of time. If you're working with a high-volume product in a call center environment, many sellers will close 10 or more contracts per day. That's 200 minutes even for a fairly efficient seller.*

That leaves you with five hours of de facto sales time. If you are currently wasting one of those hours, and you make $70,000 per year, getting rid of the time waste would make your income jump to nearly $90,000! Just by cutting down on time spent on Facebook or surfing online, you gave yourself a 28.5% salary increase.

GOOD PRACTICING TECHNIQUES

Good practicing techniques are essential for sellers of all levels. It doesn't matter for how long you have been selling or how good you are. Like any true professional, whether a top lawyer or a top athlete, sellers must improve to stay in the game—stagnation is death. If you feel on top of your game, practicing will typically be a more ad hoc affair, for example when moving from one product to another. But even on a day-to-day basis in the back of your head you should always have the question: "How can I improve?"

This typically ties in with the target tracking we have already discussed. Looking at your performance in different phases of the sales process, you should always be able to find areas to improve.

Practice remains important for seasoned sellers for another reason too. Sales is a volatile profession. The margins between success and failure are tiny; minor mood swings or changes in your own attitude can have a huge impact on your performance. Even the best of sellers will have bad days and good days—the biggest difference between an average seller and a top seller often being simply that the top seller has fewer bad days, and his bad days are often less bad than those of an average seller.

Given the small margins between success and failure, it is extremely important for sellers to have insight into their own sales process—to understand what will result in a sale and what will not. Some people are said to be born sellers, and it is true that some people have personality traits that happen to match those required in order to sell well. But without proper training and an understanding of the sales process, these sellers run the risk of suddenly "losing their mojo."

To use a sports analogy: some people are by nature good golfers. They will have walked up to the tee for the very first time, asked their caddy whether to grip the round bulky end of the club or the long narrow one and hit the ball long and straight almost immediately. Six months later they win the club championship and a year later they've turned professional. But unlike someone whose first tee shot bounced off the golf cart and rebounded into the leg of an old lady on the third tee, these people have never been forced to understand what they do right. They have never been forced to learn the technical aspects of the golf swing. They have simply never had to. If the day ever comes, and it often does, when suddenly things are not going well, they will have nothing to fall back on. That is why a good golf pro forces even the most gifted student to understand the technical aspects of the game, and that is why a good sales coach forces the most gifted sellers to understand and practice the technical aspects of selling.

Far too many team leaders, sales coaches and sales books will settle for high flying advice like "think positive," "envision your goal" and "always be closing." All good advice, but not much help if you do not have a foundation of good sales technique. Someone who does not know how to control a call, how to drive a lead toward a close or how to handle objections is not going to sell much. And if he still remains "always positive," he is quite frankly a bit of a moron.

So we practice to keep on top of our game. We practice to understand both ourselves—our weaknesses and strengths—and the technical aspect of selling. And we practice to improve our bad days, more than our best days.

In sales, practice can come in many shapes and forms. You can practice in front of the mirror while shaving or you can practice with a coach and a tape recorder. Writing down your pitch, even when you have been selling the same thing for a long time, is a good way of taking a step back and looking at your pitch in a new light. Most sellers will change their sales pitch from time to time, picking up a phrase from a colleague or testing out a new word on whim. Because the changes from call to call often are subtle, over time the pitch can change completely without the seller ever noticing it. This happens on an individual basis and it happens for whole teams. By regularly writing down the pitch, we not only make it easier for ourselves to study what we are saying and how we are selling, we also give ourselves an archive of the pitch development. If sales have gradually increased or decreased we can pull out some old pitches and see what we have changed and how this may have affected the results.

Another practice technique commonly used in sales is role play. Some sellers will do it between themselves on their own initiative; some sellers will do it together with a coach or manager. Role playing is a great way of practicing customer-seller interaction. While a written pitch or sales script is based on a presumption that every call follows a sudden logical progress, a role play allows for a wider training, developing your on-the-fly adaptation and problem-solving techniques. Still it is important to realize that role play too will often be based on certain presumptions on how a call will progress and how a customer will respond. When role playing it is therefore vital that both participants think outside the box. In addition to allow practicing the script in a more lifelike setting, role play should challenge you as a seller to think on your feet.

One great aspect of cold calling is that you will often have a nearly endless supply of people to call, provided you are willing to reduce the lead quality. If you sell ads in the Yellow Pages, you may normally call only newly started businesses or businesses that used to advertise but have not renewed their subscriptions. Such leads will normally have a higher conversion rate than a completely random call to a business that has been in operation for years. But for the training purposes, widening the source of leads may be an extremely good idea. Let's face it. Role play may be good practice, but nothing beats practicing with "live

targets." One hour on the phone with real leads will often give you more experience than days of role play. Just keep in mind that a sales pitch may need to be adapted to the lead quality. You may need to be more pushy and aggressive with bad leads, and this may backfire when you move back to calling your normal leads source, unless you pay attention to the issue and remember to readapt your pitching style.

FOCUS ON DETAILS

In my experience there are basically two schools to sales coaching. The method most commonly found is the happy-clappy, broad lines school. Coaches who swear by this method usually tell you to "think positive," "always be closing" and "have more energy." They will show you motivational videos with titles like "Secrets to Success," "Think Yourself to the Top" and similar suitably meaningless, yet positive sounding titles. As far as I am concerned, and this is where this book diverges from the mainstream literature on the subject, this is utter nonsense spread by pompous quacks. Being a good seller requires as much technical skill as being a good lawyer or a good doctor. Yet thankfully no medical college I have ever heard of will bring in new students, stick them in front of a television set and expose them to five years of "find your inner doctor" and "think yourself a surgeon" before letting them loose on the general population.

That sales coaches, even some of the most famous ones, are allowed to get away with this claptrap is degrading to the whole sales industry. It can only be based on the presumption that anyone can sell as long as he or she has enough self-confidence. No one would ever dream of presuming you can be a heart surgeon as long as you want it enough or believe enough in yourself. Yet for sales it seems a totally acceptable presumption.

The other school of thought is that sales must be thought of as a skill. Just like you need to learn the basics of electric currents and wiring if you're going to be an electrician, and just as you need to learn the law if you are going to be a lawyer, you need to learn how to sell if you're going to be a seller. No amount of happy-clappy belief in yourself, always be closing nonsense can ever compensate for a basic lack of sales skills.

I am not saying that motivational coaching does not belong in sales training. But let's be honest: a happy idiot is just an idiot who is about to be disappointed. The happy-clappy stuff it is an extra, something offered to those whose technical skills are already on a very high level. From my personal experience I have seen motivational coaching work wonders with sellers who already have the skill set to structure their conversations, handle objections well and time their closing perfectly.

So if you remember nothing else from this book, please remember this: Good selling is a talent that is taught and learned like any other talent, as a technical, a theoretical and a practical skill. There are no shortcuts. You will not become a good seller just by watching a seven-minute motivational video, by repeating a special mantra each morning or by thinking a certain thought when you walk into the office. You learn sales like you learn everything else: by studying hard and practicing.

So what details do we look for in our sales? The pitch is obviously the first place to start. The ultimate seller will practice and fine-tune every single aspect of his pitch. Every phrase, every word. He will practice his intonation and his timing. Just like a professional dancer has considered and practiced every movement, the professional seller has considered and practiced every word. Those sellers exist, and though you may not have heard of them, the world is their oyster.

Let me show you two almost similar sentences. These are the opening phrases from a pitch I was asked to refine recently:

The original opening went something like:
"Hi, my name is Jane. I'm calling from ABC Inc. You recently ordered some information regarding printing services from our website (…) Tell me a little about what sort of printing needs your company has. What business are you guys in?"
The improved opening was simply:
"Hi, my name is Jane. I'm calling from ABC Inc. You contacted us regarding the printing services we offer (…) Tell me a little about what sort of printing needs your company has. What business are you guys in?"

You may hardly notice the change at all. Yet changing the opening phrase above increased the leads-to-close ratio by 25%. Why? The original opening was fine; it kept the seller well in control, but it had one major flaw. Years of experience has taught me that if you want to close quickly, you must avoid the use of the word "information" when contacting a lead who has requested a brochure or other informational material. If you, as a seller, keep referring to "the information" the lead has ordered, it becomes very, very hard to justify a quick close. The lead will be constantly reminded about the scope of his contact with you: he just wanted to get more information. When you try to close, the immediate response is "Sure, but send the brochure first so I can have a look."

You can watch motivational videos as much as you want, but unless you treat selling as a proper skill, and handle your sales script with the same keen eye as a lawyer writing a contract or an author writing a novel, you will never be able to achieve stable, high levels of sales.

In addition to *what* you say, you need to practice *how* you say it. You don't need to have a voice suitable for professional voiceover work, but to be a good seller you must be in total command of your voice. You must know when and how to sound positive, when and how to sound surprised, when and how to sound authoritative. Practicing this is easy. Pull out a recording device—your PC or your iPhone, for example—and talk and talk. Try to emulate certain emotions through your voice. As I have mentioned above, research shows that more people can tell a lie on the phone than face to face. In my opinion this is mostly because while most people may have learned to control their faces, which dominate face-to-face interaction, few have practiced controlling their voices. For most people it simply isn't needed because face to face, the visual impact dominates.

Nothing is more painful to listen to than a seller who gets this wrong. Most painful of all is the forced excitement of a seller complimenting a client. Nothing will send a sale down the drain faster than a truly fake-sounding "Oh, that is so interesting."

A practical tip is to use facial expressions to force your voice to sound the way you want it to. Try to say "Oh, how exciting" while frowning and then say "Oh, how exciting" while smiling. You will immediately notice the difference. In fact, sounding irritated while wearing a broad smile is almost impossible. You can easily control your facial expressions (within limits at least) so use those to subconsciously control your voice. The best phone sellers in my experience are emotional: standing up, smiling when they are telling something interesting or positive, sitting down, frowning and looking very concentrated when they are discussing something serious, looking genuinely sad when the client explains a problem. It may be deliberate; it may be that it's just their nature, but the fact is that this works well to make them sound much more genuine on the phone.

HOW TO HANDLE QUESTIONS YOU DIDN'T PREPARE FOR

Preparing for questions you didn't prepare for is obviously a contradiction in terms. Yet it not only is possible, but even necessary to prepare for the unknown. It is basically called thinking on your feet, and it is a skill you can learn.

Most of the best "thinking on your feet" is in fact not thinking at all. It's just really good preparation. A politician being asked a seemingly surprise question by a journalist or a stand-up comedian being heckled by someone in the audience both coming back with perfect, coherent answers; most likely they have been asked the exact same question before. And if not, they have spent a lot of time thinking through what possible questions or comments may come and prepared a long list of answers.

Basically there are four ways of handling a question outside your normal sales script: you can try to answer truthfully as best you can, you can make something up, you can say you don't know or you can ignore the question entirely.

Except for making up an answer to a question to which you don't know the answer—which I believe should never be done—the other three options can all work well if used properly and at the right time.

> *It is not moral scruples making me warn you against just making up answers to questions. Potential customers are in general not stupid. As a seller you are often selling products to business professionals who may know, if not your product itself, then at least their industry, better than you. Combine this with the fact that (as discussed above) statistics show that people are quite good at identifying a lie on the phone, it simply isn't good sales technique to make up random answers to questions. More likely than not it will lose you the sale.*

When you decide how to handle questions, remember why you are on the phone in the first place. As a seller you are meant to sell. You are not a phone-based advertising campaign. Nor are you necessarily expected to know absolutely everything about your product. If you sell photocopiers, people will expect you to know sales-relevant details like printing speed, toner usage, color availability, networking options, price, delivery time and so on. No one, however, can realistically expect you to know whether the image sensor is a CCD or CMOS chip, what the kilowatt usage is in stand-by mode, what the operating temperature of the discharge lamp is and so on. It is obviously OK not to know the answer to such questions, yet so many sellers feel somehow that they must try to answer, and in the process end up burning the sale.

Before we look at the way of handling questions, let us also establish one other basic fact: Questions are signs of interest. If your potential customers ask questions about the product, they are probably interested! If you can handle the questions properly, they should increase your chances of a sale, not reduce them!

 So the best sellers will look at client questions as opportunities and use them to their advantage. This can mean not answering a question in a straightforward manner but rather using the question as a steppingstone to a close. Let's look at two sample sales conversations. First a traditional response:

CUSTOMER: "OK, but we have a lot of Linux-based machines in our office. Does your printer work with those machines?"

SELLER: "Yes, our software development team has just released a set of new drivers for Linux OS. This includes the latest version of Ubuntu and Red Hat. So on your Linux-based machines you will need to install those drivers, and then you install the Windows version on your Windows machines."

Compare this to the following:

CUSTOMER: "OK, but we have a lot of Linux-based machines in our office. Does your printer work with those machines?"

SELLER: "To be honest, I'll have to check up on that. I presume this is critical, practically a deal breaker for you then?"

CUSTOMER: "Yes, we won't be able to buy it without some sort of Linux compatibility."

SELLER: "OK, I'll check that with our technical department and find this out for you. Provided the printers are fully Linux compatible, which version would you be interested in—the A3 or A4 format printers? Just so I know…"

CUSTOMER: "Um, well I think we would only need the A4 printers."

SELLER: "OK, the A4 then. Just hold the line 30 seconds while I call the head of IT to discuss this with him (…) Hello? Good news, the A4 version if fully Linux compatible. In fact we just released an update to our Linux drivers, so they are fully up to date. Looking at delivery time, we normally have a four-week delivery time, but I can get that down to three weeks for you. Would that be acceptable for you guys?"

Which one of those two conversations is most likely to result in a sale? The second example is very honest—the seller simply says that he doesn't know the answer to the question and will have to check with his technical department. But at the same time he uses the question to tie down the lead. Before putting the lead on hold he prepares the lead in a way that results in a semi-commitment to buying. The lead has already indicated what model he wants to buy. When the seller returns with a positive answer, he can take it for granted that the lead is going to buy, and go straight for the closing questions.

Because the best way of handling questions may not always be a straightforward answer, I often see sellers beginning a new project and quickly getting quite good results. When they start with a new product they know very little about the product itself and must necessarily rely heavily on sales technique to get sales. As his or her knowledge of the product increases they tend to ease back on the pure sales techniques and switch to answering questions in detail. It is a human trait to want to show your knowledge. But in sales this has a tendency to blur the purpose of calls. As I pointed out above, a seller calls to sell, not to inform. Leave the information for the marketing and PR departments.

There are some questions that you simply cannot twist to your own advantage. Most of these are rhetorical of the type "Didn't we agree you'd call me next week?" or "Didn't you hear what I said? I'm not interested." A truthful answer is probably not a good idea. "Yes, I heard you but I don't really care" is not going to win you many new friends or a lot of sales. You really only have the option of ignoring the question in one way or the other. This requires a bit of practice because you need pretty good timing and a bit of guts to pull this off.

The simplest technique in these situations is just to ignore the question altogether—acting as if it was never asked. With some leads this can work quite well. But it is very easy to come off as rude or too pushy. A better way is answering the question, or at least pretending to answer the question, and immediately come back with a new question to move the lead's attention to something else:

"Didn't we agree you would call me next week?"
"Oh, perhaps we have misunderstood each other. I'm so sorry! Let me just quickly ask you a question, just for my notes: the photocopier you are using at the moment, you said it was a Canon, right? Is this a Canon DPE 5X or 6C?"

You quickly dismiss the question in a fairly neutral way and then fire back a new question. The new question is phrased in a slightly roundabout way, so the lead must focus on what you are saying and think about his answer. That way the lead tends to forget his own question, and you can move forward as if it had never been asked. Should the lead again repeat his question later ("Look, you never really answered me on my question about blah blah"), you can simply apologize and handle the question properly then. Most leads will have forgotten their questions within a few seconds if you are good at diverting their attention and then controlling the call from there.

A useful, but perhaps rather nasty, technique to use if you are asked a question you really don't want to answer is to blame the line quality:

> *"But I thought we agreed you'd send me an email with all your prices?"*
> *"Can I, hello? Um, are you… I'm sorry the line is quite bad. Can I just really quickly ask you, the printers you have today, are they all network printers or are some connected to single PCs?"*

Yes, it is crude, and no, it is not nice. But when everything else fails, this does work quite well, as long as you get your timing right. If you find yourself having to use tricks like this a lot, though, you are probably doing something else wrong. Selling well is really about controlling the conversation, and if you do that right you will rarely end up in situations where you have to fall back on this sort of tricks.

There is one situation where you should never ignore a question, and that is when the question is a clear objection, something that will obviously prevent you from closing. Leads may forget irrelevant questions like "Weren't you supposed to call me next week?" But few, if any, are so weak-minded that they will forget about something that is an absolute deal-breaker. Thus, if a client presents a question that in one way or another may come back and bite you later in the call, deal with it rather than ignoring it. Let's say you are selling printers that you fear cannot work with the potential client's internal software; don't ignore a direct question. If the lead asks "OK, it sounds good, but can your printers work with our old Amstrad printer servers?" don't pretend you didn't hear the question. You can be pretty sure this client will ask the same question again before you get him to agree to a deal. Better handle the question properly there and then. (I go into more detail about objection handling in page 131) In the end, you should also remember that selling well is not about cheating or tricking people into buying something. You are better off trying to turn the question into a closing opportunity as discussed above, saying you will check with your IT department, and then pray that your back-office staff can solve the problem, allowing you to close the deal. If they can't, in these days with increased consumer rights and potential reputation damage through Internet review sites, both you and your company are better off moving on to the next lead. After all, the main advantage of phone selling is that your time investment in each lead can be kept low.

"I told you I can't see any salesmen today!"
"He said that's fine, he's selling spectacles."

THE SALES PROCESS

THE STRUCTURE OF A SALES CALL

A standard first contact sales call has four distinct phases. Different sales literature uses different titles. I prefer to refer to them as the opening, the engager, the confirmation and the close.

The opening phase is short and brutal and is all about getting your foot in the door. All we want to focus on is getting the client to talk to us and not hang up. Mess up here and you don't even get to pitch your product. I'll be discussing cold call openings in more detail in page 67.

After we have established that the client is willing to talk to us, we move on to **the engager**. Now the client has given us some time to present ourselves and our product. Some sales books refer to this phase as the "product intro." I don't like that title at all. Phone sellers are not one-to-one radio advertisements—they should never give general product information. There is nothing more boring, dull and predictable than a seller who just starts reading out general product information here. I like to think about this phase being all about what we can do for the client. We want to tease him with some product information, but we make sure we present each product advantage in a way that is relevant to the client. Let me first exemplify with a common, average call center employee pitch:

> *"As I said, I'm calling on behalf of United Motor, one of the fastest-growing roadside assistance providers in the US. We are currently running a campaign where we offer a 30% discount on all our breakdown and roadside assistance packages for all orders placed before the end of the month."*

This is pretty much your archetypical bad phone seller pitch. The information is given in a general way, not related to the client's need. There is no attempt to show how *this* customer can benefit from *this* product. Let's look at a completely different style of pitching:

> *"Well, James, the reason I'm calling you is that I want to discuss your roadside assistance coverage. Can I just quickly ask you what model of car you own? OK, I see. And I presume it has more than 20,000 miles on the odometer too? Right. That pretty much makes you our typical customer. We are in fact the fastest-growing roadside assistance provider in the US. Do you have roadside assistance coverage today? OK, that's perfect. What I'll do for you is offer you a 30% discount on all our breakdown and roadside assistance plans, so we get that issue taken care of for you. But let me just first explain a little about what our plans actually cover…"*

That is not your average sales pitch. This is a seller who understands that in this phase the customer needs to be engaged. He asks the customer questions and uses those to present the product in a way that relates to the customer and his needs. This may sound complicated, but most questions the seller asks are there only to engage. The pitch would change very little whether the answer went one way or the other. This seller also talks about "we" to add some personality to the company he is calling from and makes sure to say things like "what I'd like to do for you" or "what I'll do for you."

If you handle the engager phase in this way, you will be able to provide all the necessary product information without the customer losing focus or hanging up. Keep the customer engaged and this phase is easy.

The confirmation phase is all about obtaining a go-ahead from the customer to move on to closing. This can take 30 seconds, it can take a few minutes or it can take 15 phone calls. The trick is to ask questions in a way that provokes the customer in one way or another to confirm that he wants the product. In this phase we are not asking direct closing questions like "Should I sign you up for a plan then?" or asking for credit cards. In this phase we just prod gently but repeatedly for a sign that we can move on. "Just so I can check availability, would you prefer red or green?" or "Does this sound good to you?" These are questions where we can reasonably justify proceeding to a proper closing, but without having popped the big question: "Do you want this?" I will be discussing various trial closing techniques in more detail in page 94.

The closing is basically where we take down the order. Sometimes you want to ask direct questions like "So, are you ready to go for this?" but in general I find that the best method is simply to start filling in your order form, asking the questions you need for that: "What would best suit your needs – a box of 12 or a box of 24?" "Can I just take down the full company name, please?" "Could I just ask you for the delivery address; what is the physical address of your office?" and so on. It makes it pretty clear that an order is being taken down, and it does make it slightly harder for customers to say "Just let me think about it." I discuss this phase in much more detail in page 92.

Understanding the different phases in a sales call is important for one major reason: you must never, ever move backward from one phase to another. You move *only* forward. So you go from the engager phase to the confirmation phase, but you never ever move from the confirmation phase to the engager phase. That is a big no-no! The phases are logically structured to tighten a mental net around the customer. As you progress through the call the customer gets caught by his own actions (basically answering your questions) and it gradually becomes more and more difficult for him to say "No I don't want to order." By letting himself be engaged in the engager phase, by giving you positive replies to the prodding questions of the confirmation phase and by answering some of the order-related questions in the closing phase, the customer attitude follows the sales pitch stages; by the end it is so obvious and natural to both of you that he is ordering, that he hopefully doesn't even consider the option of not buying.

It's a bit like the story about the frog and the hot water. Put it straight into hot water and it'll jump out. Put it in cold water and heat it gradually and it will gladly sit and let itself be boiled to death. If you start jumping back and forth between the sales phases, you break this process. If you are in the closing phase and you are asking questions like "Would you prefer delivery this month or next month?" or "I take it white is preferable to you over off-white?" and then suddenly start talking product information again, with phrases like "Our printers are the fastest on the market," you ruin the presumption that he is just naturally buying. By talking information at this stage you mentally raise the question, "Is he or is he not buying?" Giving information is your way of trying to convince the customer to buy, and as such it is also clear that you don't think he has made up his mind yet. This makes the client snap out of the presumption you have gradually built and then you will find it very hard to bring him back into it. It can no longer be taken for granted that the customer is about to buy.

So the rule is that at any time you can only ask questions belonging to the phase you are in—or move forward to the next phase. You cannot ask questions or discuss issues that belong in one of the previous stages. This goes even when the customer is (subconsciously or consciously) trying to make you do so. If you are halfway through your order form and the customer suddenly says, "You said these printers are faster than your Laser X72?" do not fall into the trap by answering something like "Yes, our range consists of the X71, X72 and the XXL. The XXL is indeed much faster than the X72." If you do that you will find that the next question from the customer may easily be something like "OK, I mean I just want to make sure that the XXL is worth the extra money. We don't actually print that much you know," and then the illusion or presumption that he was placing an order is completely broken. It is much better to simply answer "Indeed, John. I'll go through the entire specification sheet with you, but let me just take this down first. I need your full address; what is your physical office address?" That way you don't rudely dismiss the client, but you keep the focus on the order, not the general information. If the customer keeps insisting, you may of course not have any choice but to move backward. But then you need to understand the consequences and rebuild the call almost from scratch.

In my experience the most critical phase of a sales call is moving into the closing phase. This is where the majority of sales are lost. Surprisingly the most common mistake by young sellers is that they simply never get around to the closing. They may have a very good call up to this point, but feel uncomfortable moving from the information and engager phases into the proper closing. It almost appears as if they are waiting for the lead to ask if it is OK for him to buy the product or service. This, of course, rarely happens. In reality, when the information or engager phases become too long, the lead will simply say "OK, thank you for the information. You've been very helpful and I'll give you a call if I decide to buy."

Moving into closing requires a bit of guts from the seller and it requires the mental ability to think "I am not sure if this guy is really ready to buy, but I'm going to try to see if I can sell him something anyway." You'll *never* be absolutely certain that someone is ready to buy. That is not how sales works. It is your job to actively sell; those who are ready to buy will usually order online anyway. The lead may initially have said "I'm just looking for information," but that doesn't mean he is not interested in buying. After you have given him information, you still need to try to close him. If you don't try to close, you can't sell.

Because of the inherent difficulty in moving from giving information to closing the deal, some companies have decided to split the sales process. One seller will handle the opening, focusing on getting his foot in the door and arousing interest; the other will be a dedicated closer who takes the call when the information and engager phases have been completed and he simply focuses on taking down the order. The advantages of such a strategy are many: You get rid of any hesitation from the seller when he is supposed to move into closing, each seller can specialize on a smaller part of the call and the lead is usually slightly surprised when he is handed over to "an expert." In addition the lead knows that the second seller, the closer, has not heard him say "I just want information" so the closer can behave as if he presumes the lead is calling in to place an order.

MARGINS BETWEEN FAILURE AND SUCCESS IN SALES

Above we have spoken mainly about factors relating to your potential customer that can be exploited (or "used" if you prefer a more politically correct wording) to improve your sales. But there are also internal factors, factors relating to your own way of thinking and working. These, in my experience, are essential in order to succeed as a seller.

First of all, let me make one thing perfectly clear: The margins between selling and failing can be absurdly small. Since there is really just one measurement for performance in sales, that is, whether you sold or not, it can sometimes be difficult for sellers and sales managers to realize this.

Being a seller is a bit like being blind-folded and shooting a pistol at a target, only to be told whether you hit the bull's-eye or not. First of all it is difficult to know what to correct and secondly it is very difficult to know how close you are to success.

On page 31 I talk about a few things sellers can do to better set partial targets and thus measure their performance better.

Allow me to give you an example of how small the margins in sales can be. A year or so back, I was working with a seller selling a corporate product on the phone. This was a high margin product cold sold to small businesses in a massive way. The call was heavily based on a fixed sales script with very little deviation. (If you listen to the best phone sellers you will notice their calls sound amazingly similar because they are able to control the call.) An average call lasted about seven or eight minutes and at the end of the call the customer was asked to pay either by a VISA or a MasterCard. This seller had shown a nice increase in sales for some time but had now plateaued. After reviewing the seller's pitch again and again we decided to make two simple changes. Quite early on in the call the seller asked the customer what industry he was working in. We changed the wording to: "Tell me a little bit about what your company does." In addition, the seller at this point had a tendency to repeat what the customer said so you would get the customer answering "We are in the oil industry" to which the seller immediately echoed "Ah, I see, the oil industry." Instead I asked the seller to ask a follow-up question about the business activity. So before the changes a typical call would in this phase go something like this:

> *"OK, good! And tell me, what industry is your company in?"*
> *"We are in the oil industry."*
> *"Ah, I see the oil industry…"*

We now changed it to something like this:

> *"OK, good! Just for my records, and to better identify your needs, could you briefly explain what your company does?"*
> *"Sure, we are selling welding equipment to the oil industry."*
> *"Ah, OK. So we are talking about specialized equipment just for the oil industry?"*
> *"Yes, basically these are welding machines that reduce the risk of fire and explosion and (…)"*

The differences may seem minute. But those two changes alone resulted in the seller getting 50% more customers to an attempted close (here basically asking for a card number) and 25% more sales! So we can safely assume that this seller, before the changes, was very close to pulling almost all his customers all the way through his order form. The margins between getting to ask for 50 credit cards and 100 credit cards were so small that even the tiniest of change made a huge difference.

IMPROVE YOUR FOCUS TO IMPROVE YOUR SALES

Practically every field of quasi science has an 80-20 rule. I don't know why, but if you write a book about practically anything, these days, apparently you have to throw in an 80-20 rule. Apparently "20% of the world's population controls 80% of the world's income," "80% of your sales come from

20% of your clients" and surprisingly "80% of a company's complaints come from 20% of its customers." (Let's hope it's not the same 20 percent). Additionally, "80% of a company's sales are made by 20% of its sales staff" we are told (In my experience it's more 95/5.) and "20% of the hazards cause 80% of the injuries at work." These are all proper quotes from proper books. You can look them up if you want.

So I am going to throw in my own 80-20 rule of phone sales. It may be a little different, but it is no less true, I assure you: In sales, 80% focus gives you 20% of the sales.

Because of the narrow margin between success and failure in a sales call, you cannot get good results without being 100% focused. That is 100% focused, 100% of the time you pitch a customer.

Selling on the phone is an extremely intensive exercise. In a physical meeting you or the client may signal that you are unfocused or need a break. If your customer is drawing little doodle flowers in her note book or if she is typing a message on her phone, you know you can, and should, ease back a little. Similarly if you're looking through a pile of papers or trying to connect your laptop to the projector, the client will know that she can send her SMS or draw her little doodles. On the phone, however, there are no other clues than the voice. The phone is an intense medium and in general people behave, and expect you to behave, efficiently on the phone. "Hang on, I just need to look for some papers" is not a phrase you hear often on the phone. In a physical meeting it is fine (or at least lawyers and accountants seem to think so).

> *This is not to say that the client may not possibly be reading his newspaper, checking his email or drawing little doodles while you talk. But the expectation of efficiency is constantly there. On the phone a good call can turn into an ugly call so fast that only a careful analysis of the recording later may ever explain what happened.*

Business on the phone is expected to be swift and efficient and both parties behave accordingly. Therefore timing and constant control become much more important in phone selling than in face-to-face sales. If you are just a little off your game, you will lose sales and you will lose them fast.

So if you want to sell on the phone, your focus must be 100% on the call: on what the client is saying, how he says it and when he says it. And on what you are saying and are going to say a few seconds from now. Your timing must be perfect. You must know when to interrupt, when to lean back and when to take control. If you lean back at the wrong time, just pause or hesitate for a second at the critical moment, the sale will be lost. You must constantly stay ahead of the client and understand where you are in the sales call and where the call is heading. You must pick up small buying signals and anticipate potential objections— maybe just a short hesitation or a single word from the client.

PUSHING THE RIGHT BUTTONS

If you want to succeed as a seller, you must understand what generates sales, the processes that lead to the decision to buy. Decision-making theory is a complicated and perhaps a little muddled science, so I am not going to go into much detail here. Not only because a lot of it is either nonsense or long-winded explanations of the obvious, dreamed up by researches with not enough original thought and too much pressure to publish, but mostly because a lot of it is in any case irrelevant to the sales process. But there are some basics of the decision-making process of the customer that you really need to understand in order to push the right buttons as a seller.

The most essential part to understand is that a customer's decision-making process is never purely logical. That is not to say that customers are not intelligent or do not in general buy the products best suited for their needs, but that they don't follow a purely logical process when making decisions. For this very reason, sellers who try to over explain their products, pouring out details about why their products are the best choice, tend to fail. In fact pouring out arguments, no matter how positive, has a tendency to lead to **analysis paralysis**. This is a much-studied state of mind where the number of details the customer is exposed to simply overloads his or her mind, resulting in over-thinking the decision. As a result the customer, although he might think the product is great, is unable to reach a decision. And in sales a "maybe" is as useful as a "no."

Let's look at this another way: Let's, for the sake of argument, say that you are selling printers. Now some level of product information is obviously required for a sale. You may want to explain that the printer can print 50 sheets per minute, that it offers both black-and-white and color printing and that it is very economical—all essential information for a potential client. Now, however, let's say that you have been selling this product for years, you are married to the inventor's daughter or you are just overly keen to show off your knowledge. So in addition to the above facts, you start explaining that the printer operates at only 53 decibels, that it uses only 1000 kilowatt-hours per year, that it in addition to duplex printing it can also do four pages per sheet automatically in economy mode, that the main chip is made under license from a US firm and so on. Logically all this could have been pieces in a larger logical puzzle that eventually would make the potential customer scream, "Stop, you have convinced me. I will buy!" In the real world, however, the result is that the customer's mind starts spinning. Because for each good argument you have mentioned, you have also given the customer one more thing to think about. "I don't know how much a dB is; is 53 of them good or bad? Does the newest Samsung printer make more than 53dB noise, or less, and if so, how much less? And is 1000 kilowatt-hours a lot? Should I check this first? How much does a kilowatt-hour cost? Is this going to be cheap or expensive to operate? Are there cheaper printers available? What the hell is duplex printing? Do I need it? And if the chip is made under license, perhaps I should buy a printer from a company that has its own license. What is a chip? What is a chip license anyway?" the customer might think before his brain shuts down for essential repair and maintenance. By pouring out information you have lost the sale to a lead who might have otherwise bought.

I see information overload a lot; it is an odd phenomenon because it tends to occur more the keener and more experienced the seller is. You would think that experienced and keen sellers would sell more, and of course in general they do. But many regretfully fall into this trap, at least for a while, resulting in a drastic reduction of sales.

Information overload can occur both from the amount of information loaded on the customer and from the type of information. A little, but very complex information, may do more damage than a lot of simple information. Some information is easily absorbed because we are so used to dealing with it. Mentioning color range by color name, for example, will do much less damage than starting to ramble off color codes or hexadecimal process colors. One of the things I always tell my sellers is that numbers are in general a big no-no except for the price. If you need to quantify something, quantify it by words. "Very quiet" is much easier for a potential customer to digest than "53dB" (which for a printer is in fact very quiet). Likewise, "very light" is much easier to understand and poses less risk of information overload than "5.35 kilograms."

In a now famous experiment, Sheena Iyengar, a professor at Columbia University, tested consumer response to quantitative differences in jam variety (a fancy way of saying that she tested how consumers' behavior changed depending on the number of jams offered). At a luxury food store in Menlo Park, the researchers set up a table offering samples of jam. Sometimes there were six different flavors to choose from. At other times there were 24. The study concluded that although shoppers were more likely to stop by the table with more flavors, after the taste test, those who chose from the smaller number were ten times more likely to actually buy jam: 30 percent versus three percent. Having too many options, too much to think about, made it hard for the shoppers to decide, and in the end they bought nothing.

There are a few other biases in the decision-making process that you as a seller should be aware of. The first is often referred to as **recency**. People in general tend to place more weight on more recent information. This is one of the reasons selling quickly is important. If a customer is going to "think about it," chances are that he or she will speak to someone else (another seller, a friend or family member) and be told something else. This ties in with another general bias referred to as **source credibility bias:** we generally put more trust in people we like or relate to, even if they may have less knowledge of the product. This latter bias is something most sellers have experienced and been puzzled by. You find a customer who clearly will benefit from your product, you explain it well to her, she seems keen and then when you call her back the next day she has spoken to her mother/father/sister's friend who is a dentist/her school teacher/her accountant and is definitely not interested because (select person from above list) said that printer fumes are dangerous/printers are about to be outlawed/typewriters are better/printers are a waste of money when you can buy a pen for 35 cents. I will talk more about how you as a seller can create trust and build credibility to combat this in page 140.

Another, more useful decision-making bias is **repetition.** Basically people will believe anything if it is repeated often enough. For you as a seller that is generally a good thing. If you keep hammering away on that stubborn customer, chances are you will get there in the end (although you should probably have sold on the first call and saved yourself a lot of work).

Anchoring bias refers to a theory that people have a slight tendency to be more influenced by initial information since that information shapes your whole view of a subject. This is obviously hard to reconcile with the recency bias mentioned above, but to a certain degree all people are exposed to both biases at the same time. While the recency bias tends to be most efficient when relating to minor information and details, the anchoring bias tends to have most effect when it relates to information that shapes our understanding of a whole concept or situation. The policeman who is told by a crying woman that she was just robbed by person X in the street just around the corner from the grocery will use that information to shape a mental picture of the situation and that picture tends to stay with the policeman for some time. Even if person X insists that he "ain't done nothing wrong" there is a tendency for such information to be dismissed since it doesn't fit with the police officer's mental image of the incident.

> *Police officers are, in fact, trained to handle this and other types of bias and to try to overcome their tendency to believe some people more than others. This was just an example to illustrate how anchoring bias works.*

 Group bias is another example of factors that have a strong influence on how we behave as consumers and buyers. This often takes the shape of peer pressure (e.g. All my friends have bought an SUV so I must too…) but on a smaller scale it can be used by you as a seller. If you can relate a product to a person the customer may know of ("In fact, we just sold one of our cash registers to Darcy's Hair Studio. Just down the street from you, I think…), it may work to your advantage.

 Self bias (or "attribution asymmetry" as it is often referred to in decision-making theory) is another important factor when a potential customer is making up his mind. In general a person tends to think he is better than he is. Particularly successful people tend to attribute their success to internal factors (their own abilities) rather than external factors such as luck, a big inheritance and so forth. Knowing this, as a seller, can be helpful because you can pamper to the person's need for self-assertion. If you're working with customers higher up the social or corporate ladder, it is important to make sure the decision to buy appears to be the customers' own. Phrases like "I fully understand why you contacted us" and "I agree with you that this certainly seems to be the best product for you" usually work well.

Sunk cost is another factor that can influence a potential customer's decision-making process. Most people have a tendency to favor options they have already invested time or money in, even if those options from a logical perspective seem less favorable. As a seller you can use this to your advantage in several ways. One way is to get in contact with the customer at an earlier stage than your competition. If the customer has spent time discussing and planning your solution, it is less likely that he will go with another option later. In addition, you can also get a customer to sign up by structuring the investment in steps. The first investment may seem minimal to the client, but if the investment has first been made, he or she will tend to favor your solution over other alternatives.

GETTING YOUR FOOT IN THE DOOR

Getting your foot in the door (literally in an office or meta-phorically on the phone) is the classic problem for any seller. A lot has been written about how to do this, but let's be honest: The best way of getting your foot in the door is to be invited in first. It sounds obvious, but for one reason or another so many people—both professional sellers and others—forget this. By preparing well, you can change a potential cold call to an invitation.

First of all, you should always look for a way of getting a referral. A referral changes the aspect of the initial phase of the call completely. How much easier than a complete cold call is the start: "John, hi, this is George Anderson. Peter Johnson at Haircuts4You suggested I call you about your photocopier. He said you guys have been having some problems with your current supplier?"

There are of course about a million different ways of getting referrals. But they all have one common factor: You have to ask for them. You may spend years selling on the phone before someone is going to say, "No, honey, I don't need a photocopier. I'm 94 years old, you know. But you should call my doctor, John Johnson. He might need one."

Always, always ask for a referral before terminating the call. Did the client buy from you? Perfect. When the contract is signed, simply say, "Oh, by the way, Peter, now when we've got your photocopier sorted out, you surely must have some friends who need help with their copiers too?" The client didn't buy? Ask nonetheless. What do you

have to lose by trying: "OK, sure Peter, I understand. If it's OK I'll give you a call in six months' time to see if your situation has changed. By the way, Peter, even if we couldn't help you right now, I am sure you have some friends or acquaintances who do need some help with their copiers, though, right?" So what if he thinks you're a little pushy. The client didn't buy. Nine out of ten might say, "Sorry, I don't," but if you can get a hot-ish lead for every ten failed call, you're still going to be laughing. Even if you get just one referral in 5,000 calls, it's still worth doing. You have nothing to lose and everything to gain.

These are basically free potential customers. Good, free potential leads. You have established they probably need the product you're selling, and you have the perfect opening to the call by mentioning the referral. Yet do I hear most sellers do this? "No," I hear the voices in my deranged head whisper.

And they're right. Every time I coach a new team of sellers, regardless of their experience or performance, I have to explain the power of referrals to them. A few days later they tell me "Wow, this really works" and when I come back three months later they've forgotten all about asking for referrals and can't for the life of them figure out why their sales have dropped back.

So if you want to be a top seller, not just a good one, but one of those few who seem to have a magical touch with clients and is sought after by practically any corporation under the sun, start by tattooing "Don't forget referrals" in high visibility ink on the back of your hand so you can see it just in time before hanging up.

PURE COLD CALL OPENERS

Pure cold calling is the life and blood of the phone sales industry. Cold calling utilizes the main strength of phone selling: the sheer volume of people you can reach. A predictive dialer can easily dial 600 or more numbers per agent, and an efficient phone seller on such systems can talk to perhaps more than 100 people in a day. Compared to traditional face-to-face sales, where a seller can rarely manage more than a handful of meetings in a day, the advantages are huge.

When cold calling, though, you are faced with one major problem: most people are weary of phone sellers and do not really want to talk to you. This is understandable, of course. Phone sellers rarely call at very convenient times (mostly because there is no particular part of the day where a normal human being has so little to do that talking to a phone seller is on the top of his to-do list), most people you reach will not be interested in your product, and in addition a lot of phone sellers are sadly terrible at their jobs and a pain to listen to.

As a phone seller you need to understand and respect people's attitudes toward you. In the same way an advertising executive accepts that most people who sees his advertisement will not be interested in the product, you as a phone seller must accept that most people you call will not be interested either in you or your offer. The important thing is to get your message across, so that the potential customer can make a fairly intelligent decision on whether she is interested or not.

Here we are touching on something essential (although obvious). The aim of the opening is to get your basic message across. Sadly a lot of sellers misunderstand this and think that the purpose is to talk to every customer at any cost. They will come up with elaborate, roundabout openings, just to get the client to talk to them. Some try to hide the fact that they are selling, some try some shocking opener, some again turn into amateur stand-up comedians.

Let's try some simple mathematics here. Seller A has a long, fancy opening pitch. He talks and talks, just to keep the customer on the line, because his biggest fear in the world is getting a "no" early on in the call. Because he hardly gives the customer a chance to say anything during the first few minutes, and because the customer really doesn't understand why he is calling, he spends an average of two minutes on each call. Seller B has a much more straightforward pitch. He gets his message across quickly and efficiently. Because of this, his average call time is only 45 seconds. Both sellers convert 5% of their calls into sales. Look at these figures now. Seller B will talk to 2.5 times as many leads as seller A every day. Who do you think takes home the bigger pay check?

Spending more time on a lead can be justified only if it results in a sufficient increase in conversion. That requires you to spend those extra seconds or minutes at the right time, with the right customer. Spending significantly more time with every single person you call is not the way to go.

So, to conclude: When cold calling, our aim is not to get to talk to every lead, but to get to sell to the right leads. Your opening should get your message across efficiently and in a way that makes the wrong leads hang up and the right leads stay on.

There is a school of sellers, though "school" may not be the right word for such nitwits, who seem to think it's a great idea to call and pretend they are doing anything but selling. This seems particularly popular among sellers of advertising space in newspaper insert magazines, who will, for reasons known only to them and their incompetent sales coaches, pretend to call as journalists. They will say they are doing articles about something related to the lead's industry, and ask seemingly genuine questions for the article. After wasting anything from 15 minutes to several days of the lead's time, they will eventually, in an extraordinary roundabout way, mention that they are in fact selling advertising space next to the article. When the lead invariably gets upset, they will even hint that the bigger advertisement you buy the more influence you will have on the article, and no advertisement may lead to an inconvenient mentioning of the lead's business in the article. I have not yet met any seller using this technique who drives a Porsche or owns a big yacht. I have, however, met one who had his nose broken by an angry lead who spent two days writing down articulate and intelligent answers for the "article."

Another school of sellers swear to the equally unsuccessful shock-opening technique. I particularly recall a young gentleman selling advertisements for a Police Dog magazine. He used to open every call with: "Hello, this is from the police. May I speak to Mr. John Doe, please." He is currently in jail.

I am not saying that you should start every call by saying "Hi, I'm calling to sell you a new photocopier. Are you interested?" Every phone seller needs to use some finesse to get his foot in the door—just enough to present his product. But it does mean that you should be fairly direct. And you should definitely not be pretending that you are not a seller.

When you open a complete cold call, you should always try to include a reference to something noteworthy about the lead or his company if you have that information: "Mr. Robertson, this is Joe Anderson. I'm calling from Copiers4You. I understand you are currently working with Pogo City Council; is that correct?" By referring to something you know about his or her current work, you grab attention and make the person listen. Also by phrasing it as a question, you force the lead's focus from how to get rid of you to answering your question. All this makes it less likely he or she will hang up immediately.

If you know nothing about the lead (Let's presume, for example, that you are working on a project with a high call volume), I find that the easiest opening is the most straightforward. "Mr. Robertson, this is Joe Anderson. I understand you run Robertson Accounting Services and I'd like to talk with you regarding reducing your photocopier costs." There! You've said it. You've got the most difficult part of the opening out of the way: you have identified yourself as a seller and you've identified what you are selling.

Now there are basically two ways of following that. You can either go straight on to a question or you can fight your main battle right away. Let's look at the question option. Basically you open with something like "Mr. Robertson, this is Joe Anderson. I understand you run Robertson Accounting Services and I'd like to talk with you regarding reducing your photocopier costs. I understand you have the Xerox ETC 1209 today, is that correct?" It is of no consequence whether you know this or not. The whole point is again, as above, to use the question to distract the lead enough to prevent him saying "get lost" right away. I find that this tactic works well for newer sellers or if you are having a bad day. It is easy to replicate in call after call, and you will get your foot in the door in a fair number of calls, even if your timing isn't perfect. Hopefully the lead will answer either "Yes we do" or "No we don't." The next few sentences play out the same way regardless of the answer. The only difference is that if the customer confirms that it is indeed the copier they have, you say "Exactly, and as you know the operating costs of the ETC 1209 are more than 30% higher than some modern solutions." If the client says "No, we have the IBM TU2" you play it the same way with "Ah, the TU2! Good thing I called you today then since you know the operating costs of the TU2 are more than 30% higher than some modern solutions." Should the potential client say "I don't know what copier we have," you can simply say "Ah! You're not alone! Lots of people don't know the brand of copier they use, even if some copiers can cost more than 30% more to operate than the most efficient machines." In either case you follow immediately with a question to keep engaging the lead. With this simple technique you have achieved three essential things: you have gotten your foot in the door by making the client talk to you, you have said who you are and you have said why you are calling. To get those latter two issues out of the way this early in the call gives you a cleaner pitch. Sooner or later you must tell the lead anyway; you can't close a deal without the lead realizing you are selling something.

Now option two, as I mentioned above, is to fight a small battle with the lead right here in the opening. If you *don't* ask a question immediately in the opening, there really is only one way for the lead to respond and that is to tell you he or she is not interested:

> "Mr. Robertson, this is Joe Anderson. I understand you run Robertson Accounting Services and I'd like to talk with you regarding reducing your photocopier costs."
> "Yes, um, we're not interested."

The words may vary but the essence is invariable. Anyone above the age of two knows that if he answers anything other than "not interested" it will at best result in 40 minutes wasted on the phone, at worst a $75,000 investment in an industrial copier he doesn't need. In general I tell my sellers to stay proactive and do what they can to prevent the customer from getting to say "not interested." It is one thing having the lead thinking "I don't want this," and a completely different thing for him to say it out loud. Then he is committed. Here, however, we are barely five seconds into the call and neither seller nor lead feels committed by what is said in this early phase. It is simply considered a standard opening for a sales call: the lead feel that he is expected to say no in this stage, almost as part of the game (like a street vendor trader with a pushcart expects you to haggle).

Thus some sellers allow the client to say "no thanks" at this stage, and then fight a short battle to still get their foot in the door. For the best sellers this sometimes works really well:

"Mr. Robertson, this is Joe Anderson. I understand you run Robertson Accounting Services and I'd like to talk with you regarding reducing your photocopier costs."
"Yes, um, we're not interested."
"That is OK. In fact that is exactly why I'm calling you: to arouse your interest. No need to be afraid; I'm a professional and know what I'm doing. Tell me...your current copier, do you know how old that is?"

This has one major advantage: The lead has had his chance; he said his meek "no," you said "don't worry" and basically just ignored him. What has happened then is that roles and a hierarchy have been established. If the lead lets you get away with this—and if your timing and voice are perfect most will—then he or she has been reduced to a listener. You are the expert; you are the one in charge. This makes the rest of the sales call easier. The drawback is that if you try this opening and you're not good enough (either you lack practice or you are just having a bad day), then you will burn a lot of leads. If you sound insecure or hesitant or if your timing is just a little bit off, you will be told to get lost by a large majority of leads even before you're 20 seconds into the call.

Either of these openings will clear many initial obstacles and set things up for a clean, well-controlled pitch. Because you use a uniform opening, you can use your sales technique to control the call into a uniform sales pitch. That way you will know exactly where you are in your calls, what you will say next and what objections are likely to be encountered.

If, however, you decide to get too creative and less direct in your openings, like many inexperienced sellers, you set yourself up for a messy call, with many potential objections:

SELLER: Hi! Is this Jane?

CUSTOMER: Yes?

SELLER: Hi Jane! This is Peter. I just wanted to check with you: Your copier is working fine now?

CUSTOMER: Yes, it's working fine. Are you from the service and maintenance company?

SELLER: Um, no. I mean, we do offer copiers and copier maintenance.

CUSTOMER: Are you calling to sell me something?

SELLER: No! Definitely not. I just want to give you some information about the services and products we offer...

And so on. Saying "No, I'm not selling anything" is, by the way, the surest way of not selling anything. Yet I hear it from inexperienced sellers all the time. Somehow many young sellers think that they must hide the fact that they are selling at any cost.

Regardless of what strategy you choose for your initial contact, be prepared to meet some objections fairly quickly. You can read about objection-handling strategies in page 113.

"Don't let me frighten you into a hasty decision.
Sleep on it tonight. If you wake in the morning, give me a call
and we'll arrange for your supplement subscription."

CONTROLLING THE CALL

THE IMPORTANCE OF CONTROLLING A SALES CALL

If you wanted to ride a horse from point A to point B, most people would realize they would have to control the horse. If the horse was left alone to control the journey you would most likely end up where the horse wanted to be, not where you wanted to be. But when asked to call a customer with the specific purpose of reaching a target such as booking a meeting or closing a deal, many new sellers seem to think that it is OK to lean back and let the call take its own course.

Let's first establish one simple fact: If people wanted to buy on their own, if they were ready to pull out their checkbooks, the world wouldn't need sellers.

> *So, a little tip to file under the happy-clappy category: Every time you are up against one of those hard leads that cost you hours of work and seem impossible to convert, be grateful. They are the reason why the sales profession exists. And what a sad place the world would be without sellers.*

As a seller, your job is basically to gently nurture the seeds of interest. You do that through good, discrete sales technique and good control of the conversation. Good selling is not like in the movies. A good seller does not argue with superior logic, a good seller does not get a "no" and then argue so brilliantly that eventually the customer throws up his hand and says "I'm convinced! Where do I sign?" When you listen to the best sellers, the million-dollar sellers, you won't even know that they are selling. Every call will just flow the way the seller planned and wanted. Instead of handling objections, the top sellers avoid objections, prevent objections from ever occurring. And instead of being pushy, trying to actively convince customers to buy, top sellers make the customers convince themselves.

As we touched on in page 65, getting the start of any call right is essential to establish and maintain control of the conversation. Just as first impressions are essential to face-to-face meetings, the first few seconds of a call establish a relationship between you and the lead and shape the rest of the call. If you have established yourself as the person in charge of the conversation at this point, you are ahead of the game. On the other hand, if you have let the client take control at this point, you might as well hang up. You will never be able to regain control once the relationship between you and the client has been established with him in control.

Having successfully taken control of the opening phase, the successful seller will maintain that control without the lead ever realizing it. The conversation just flows naturally, without the seller forcing it. And a good seller definitely doesn't seem pushy or rude.

The easiest way to maintain control of a conversation is by asking questions. If you end a sentence with a question, people will almost always automatically answer it rather than saying what they were planning to say a second before (quite often something involving being "very busy right now").

Using questions to control a call toward your ultimate goal, whether it is closing a sale or booking a meeting, is the only way you can hope to achieve what you want. No—absolutely no—sentence should come out of your mouth without a question at the end unless you are absolutely positive the other person is agreeing with you and is doing the closing for you.

Questions work in sales because questions by their very nature require answers. Not answering a question is rude, and most people do not want to come off as rude, even to a total stranger. People are in any case so programmed to answer questions that it happens without thinking. This gives you a huge advantage in a call since while you act and steer the conversation, the lead is left just reacting. In such a pattern it becomes extremely hard for a lead to ever regain control.

This principle of action and reaction is often referred to as a Boyd Loop, named after the military strategist John Boyd.

THE BOYD LOOP AND CONTROLLED QUESTIONING

The principle of the Boyd Loop is simple: Although two people enter an interaction (a conversation, a negotiation or even a fight) with different plans and strategies, as soon as the interaction starts a correlation develops where person A does X, which makes person B do Y, which again makes person A do Z and so on. Here both parties are basically reduced to reacting to the other person. If person A is able to break the loop ("get on the inside of B's loop"), she can take control of the interaction and act, rather than react. This break of the loop puts person B into a situation where he is behind and must react to person A only, just to stay in the game. Person A has taken the initiative and can control the outcome of the interaction.

The Boyd Loop theory is used by top lawyers in litigation and by the best business negotiators. *And* in sales by the absolute elite of sellers. The main tool they use to achieve this is asking questions.

I'm boring you with theory here because it is important. The aim of the questions you ask must be to either break a Boyd Loop or maintain control of a Boyd Loop. Only when you understand the purpose of the questions will you understand what questions will work to your advantage.

First of all: Certain question-like sentences are not proper questions. "John, I gather from this you are interested in a new printer," is a statement. It is *not* a question. More to the point, it doesn't force John subconsciously to answer in any specific way. Therefore it is useless in order to gain control over a conversation. John may respond "Yes! I need 500 printers by tomorrow," but John may also respond, "Who are you calling from again?" or simply "I'm sorry, I'm busy at the moment."

In order to break a Boyd Loop, a question must be so direct and clear that the customer answers without thinking. It must push those buttons that force the customer into subconsciously formulating a reply in his mind, instead of thinking about what he was actually planning to say. In addition the question must have a certain level of complexity in order for the customer to focus on it. "How are you, John?" may be a question, but unless there is something seriously wrong with John, his mind will be capable of preparing both the reply "good" and the follow-up "but, I'm a little busy now."

Questions that can be answered with a simple "yes" or "no" serve little purpose when it comes to taking control of a conversation. Multiple choice questions such as "Do you prefer white or yellow" may be a little better, but again they may not engage the client sufficiently to secure control. It is simply too easy for a potential customer to answer, "White, but listen, I'm really busy now. Can you call me next week?" And that is bad. Really bad. Because what just happened there is that the customer got on the inside of your loop. Now you are forced to react in one way or another. You can ignore the question, you can answer, you can beg. Whatever you do, though, it is a reaction to the customer's action and you are now behind. The control has been lost.

The best questions are usually "tell me" questions. Somehow our brains seem programmed to snap to attention as soon as a question starts with "tell me." Try it yourself if you want to. "Do you like red?" Nothing. But say "Tell me, what color car do you prefer?" and the brain immediately starts focusing on the question. Most likely it is simply tied to experience. We know that when someone says "tell me" it is usually a serious question and we need to focus to reply.

Some questions are big no-nos. In sales any question starting with "Why...?" are generally considered bad. "Why can't you make a decision today?" "Why do you need to see a brochure when I can answer all of your questions?" "Why have you limited yourself to such a narrow range of options?" There is something about the question "Why...?" that to most people just sounds irritating. Most "why" questions we are asked, from childhood, have some sort of hidden accusation: "Why are you late?" "Why do you talk like that?" In general people simply react negatively to even the most innocent of "why" questions. If you find yourself asking many "why" questions, you should think through your whole pitch. A sales pitch that flows well needs no "why" questions.

Questions should stay positive and try to engage the client positively. Be careful not to ask questions that may put the client in a difficult or embarrassing situation. You should either know the answer or know that the answer does not matter to your sales pitch. Here are some examples of the wrong sort of questions:

SELLER: *"OK, so tell me, how much do you turn over in your company?"*
CUSTOMER: *"Nothing, we're not starting up our business until next month."*

CUSTOMER: *"No, don't call on Friday. Next Tuesday is better."*
SELLER: *"Ah! Taking a long weekend. Are you going anywhere fun?"*
CUSTOMER: *"It's my father's funeral."*

SELLER: *"So how much do you expect your turnover to grown next year?"*
CUSTOMER: *"Well, we actually just lost our biggest client and are letting go of nearly half the staff."*

And, *halfway through a credit card number to secure an order, my favorite of all times:*
SELLER: *"OK, so that is 4755 2090... Wow, there is a lot of noise at your end now. Is there an ambulance behind your car?"*
CUSTOMER: *"No, I'm a paramedic and we're on our way to an accident now. Maybe it'll be easier if I call you on Monday when it's a little quieter?"*

Again: The golden rule is that you should either know the answer to the questions you are asking or you should know that the answers don't matter. You can easily make most questions safer just by rewording them slightly. "What is your turnover?" is risky unless you know the lead's business is doing well. A safer question is "How much do you hope to turn over in your business within the next five years?" Many people can turn over almost nothing, but few people will be hoping to turn over nothing five years from now. "When should I call you?" is risky because you and the customer may not have the same expectations at all when it comes to how quickly you should be concluding a deal. I don't know how many sellers' faces I have seen drop when the "good lead" they had expected to close within a day or two suddenly answered "Call me next January. We'll be ready to make a decision then." Much safer to say "I'll give you a call tomorrow. When is it convenient for you for me to call?" or the even safer "I'll give you a call tomorrow. I've got a canceled meeting at 5:30. Is that OK for you?"

In general you should avoid any question that focuses on you rather than on the client. Such "me" questions seem obnoxious and can easily put a client in an uncomfortable situation. "Have you heard of us?" or "What do you know about our company?" are exactly such questions. They break the flow of the call by moving the focus away from what really matters: the customer and his needs. And they often result in the lead feeling embarrassed because he had to admit he knew nothing. If you have to use such questions make sure you don't leave them hanging, pushing the client to answer. "I don't know how much you know about our color laser printers, but just to explain shortly (…)" is a safe alternative. You open for the lead to make any sort of sound to acknowledge that he is familiar with the product, but if he doesn't you just keep moving forward with the call.

Not everything we say as sellers can be a question. But again the purpose of questions in a sales call, breaking the Boyd Loop, means that we need to emphasize our questions. We do this by timing and by *always* putting the questions at the end of the sentence. Don't say "I don't know if you prefer white or yellow. Our printers come in both colors." Say "Our printers come in both white and yellow. What color do you prefer? White or yellow?" Here we have also used an efficient technique of adding the same or a similar question in a short form right at the end. I know I said

above to avoid multiple choice questions, but sometimes you really want to focus the customer's attention on a specific question. Repeating the options like this, just after the question, has a tendency to lead to a quick, almost reflex-like, reply from the customer and can be very useful in critical phases of the call.

Your questions should *always* remain professional. Do not ask questions about the weather, family or hobbies. The days when sellers could sell by knowing the name of the customer's wife and children, and opening calls with "How's little Anne doing? Did she enjoy your holiday to Arizona?" are long gone. Today, and more so on the phone than with any other medium, there is an expectation of efficiency and professionalism. Step outside this, and you will find sales your sales dropping.

Finally we never, never ask negative questions—questions where we expect and anticipate a negative answer. We do *not* ask "It wouldn't be convenient for me to call tomorrow, would it?" or "You haven't made a decision yet, have you?" We ask positive questions: "Is 5 PM tomorrow convenient for you?" or "Have you had a chance to make a decision yet?" Life as a seller is hard enough without your practically begging for negative answer. People prefer to please and hate to disappoint and the more they feel that you expect one answer, the more they will try to avoid giving you something else. But if they see an opening like a question of the type "you wouldn't, would you?" they will take it.

As you move through your pitch, the nature of your questions should change. In the opening phase the main aim of the questions is to get the client to talk rather than hang up. In this phase you want to stick to simple and nonthreatening questions. Questions should be relatively broad and unspecific in this stage, but not so general they become meaningless. Don't ask silly questions like "So, I guess you have printers, right?" and don't ask such inquisitive questions the potential customer becomes nervous, like "How many users do you have per network printer today and what is the average sheet print volume per user per day?" In this phase you want to get the conversation flowing with questions that encourage dialog within reason. Don't leave your questions so open the customer doesn't really know what to answer. A good balance would be something like "Tell me a little bit about your printer situation today; do you use desktop or network printers?"

As you progress through your call you want to get the customer to open up a bit more and you probably need more complex information for your actual sale (either to start preparing an order form for those quick sales or to identify the right product to sell to this customer).

This is a quite sensitive phase. If you become too inquisitive too soon, the client may get spooked and hang up or ask you to call back some other time. This happens amazingly fast. Even the most experienced seller will sometime feel she has a really good call going and then suddenly, boom, the lead hangs up or gets very distant and cold, leaving the seller thinking "What the heck happened there?" What happened is most likely that you got your questions wrong; you asked a too detailed, too complex or too intrusive question too soon.

This, by the way, is why sellers should record as many calls and as much of calls as possible (and as allowed by law). Only by analyzing the recordings later will you be able to find out exactly where you went wrong. And if you don't find out what you did wrong you can't fix it. Listen to the customer's voice and try to judge his level of keenness (how warm the lead is). If reviewed thoroughly enough you will almost always be able to identify what went wrong and where it went wrong.

Planning the order of your questions requires a good deal of strategy. This is why we always want to have a written, pre-planned script for every call. You need to know exactly what question to ask at what stage of the conversation. Some questions obviously belong to either the opening or the closing phase of the call. You don't ask for a credit card number within the first 30 seconds for example, and you don't end a call by asking "Is this John Johnson?" But in between those extremes there is a range of questions that need to be arranged in the right order, starting with the easy, general ones, and ending with the specific, complex and sensitive questions. You simply cannot do that successfully off the top of your head, no matter how good you are.

In every phase of the call, make sure your questions flow freely and sound natural. You do not want the customer to feel he is being interrogated. Here some adjustment may be needed from call to call. If your customer is talkative and friendly, he may just need the gentlest of prodding from time to time: "Really? And do you use desktop printers today?" "So only network printers, then?" But if your customer is a silent, grumpy type of person who responds to questions with just a single word, you may need some fillers so you don't end up with something like this:

"Do you use desktop printers today?"
"Yes."
"How many?"
"Eight."
"Do you know the brand?"
"Canon."

These may not be bad leads or bad calls. Some people simply do not like to talk and you can still sell to them, while others love to talk but may still be impossible to close. But if people do not volunteer much information, you need to work a bit to make sure the call doesn't become a ping-pong match where you ask a single question and the customer answers in a single word. You can use filler sentences and you can, and should, ask follow-up questions to learn more.

Try to word questions so that the client is forced to talk a bit more. The call could have gone something like this:

"Do you use desktop printers today?"
"Yes."
"Ah, great! Tell me, do you know how many such desktop printers are in use in your office today?"
"Eight."
"I see! And are any of these set up for network printing too. I mean, tell me a little bit more about your office printer setup in general."
"Well, um, I think we only use individual printers. One for each PC."
"Ah, good thing I called you today, then. Network printing can really save you a lot in terms of both hardware investment and operating costs. I guess all your PCs are connected to the Internet, right?"

And so on. Suddenly the conversation flows much more naturally and the customer doesn't feel he is being the subject of a third-degree interrogation.

LISTEN AND ANTICIPATE POTENTIAL PROBLEMS

Selling is not something that is done in a vacuum. Unlike some jobs, you are not solely directly in control of the outcome. If you're a bricklayer and you do a good job, you will build a good wall. In sales the "bricks" talk back to you and sometimes they just run off. Being a good salesman is about staying alert and in as much control as you can and about preempting potential problems. A good salesman will know the signs of a "brick" about to run off and he will know what to do about it.

To think that sales is a one-sided thing that you "do" to the lead is extremely dangerous. It is as absurd as a chess player playing his game without caring what moves his opponent makes. Yet I am constantly surprised by how many sellers, even intelligent sellers, think that all they have to focus on is their own pitch.

Even if you feel you are in total control of the call, active listening with 100% attention is vital. If you don't, people will very quickly realize it, either because you ask a question they've already answered earlier in the call or because you make a statement that contradicts information they have provided— or simply because when you don't listen properly your pace and timing doesn't match that of a normal conversation. And if people feel you are not listening, they also feel that you don't care about them or their interests. And who wants to do business with someone who doesn't care?

Not listening actively will also make you miss buying signals, things that the person says that you could use to close a sale or an agreement immediately. Likewise you may miss obstacles and objections that you must deal with in order to progress to the closing phase.

And finally, if you don't listen you won't have any idea what the other person is thinking or—if on the phone—doing. Is he reading the newspaper or checking his email or is he actually paying attention to you?

So from this we can deduce that when you are listening to the other party in a sales conversation or a negotiation what you want to listen for falls into three separate categories: mood, obstacles and objections, and buying signals.

Understanding the other party's mood is vital for your timing and your pitch. It is primarily the mood that will help you know how quickly you can move from simple, easy questions to the more complex and difficult ones—from one phase of the call to the next.

When you are in a meeting you can judge someone's mood from how he or she behaves: Is she looking you in the eyes, is she fiddling with his mobile phone? On the phone, however, all you have to go by is her voice. Does she sound interested? Does she answer quickly and with meaningful sentences? If the potential customer started off answering with full sentences and now is just answering with "aha" and "mm" noises, you can be pretty sure you are losing her.

Other indications that you are losing a lead's attention—and losing the deal—are keyboard chatter in the background and pauses between your questions and the person's answers. He may easily have put you on a speaker and be doing something completely different, like eating his lunch or reading his emails. As soon as you get any indication that you are losing the other lead's attention, get it back immediately!

The founder of one of the biggest call centers in Europe—who was just another seller (albeit a great one) when I first met him many years back—told me he always tried to form a mental image of what the person on the other end of the line was doing. Is she listening and taking notes? Is she writing an email to someone else while you talk or is she making coffee? If you can envision what the other person is doing, you can also prevent problems and get her attention back at the right time. It is also a technique that helps you focus on the call and not your colleagues or emails.

Listening for obstacles and objections is important because you need to know they are there and overcome them before you close a deal. Objections can come in every phase of the sales call, though they mostly occur during the opening phase and as you move into the closing phase.

Instead of looking at objections as a negative thing—something that can prevent a deal—the best sellers look at objections as a great way of closing. Objections are often actually the customer saying "I'm interested but…," and if you can solve that "but" you will have a deal. I have devoted a whole chapter (page 113) to objection handling, so I won't go into much detail here. However, when it comes to the listening bit, we should draw a line between potential showstoppers and what I like to call "theatrical" or false objections. Showstopping objections are of a type that makes it impossible to close. "We already have a printer service deal we are quite happy with" or "Our current supplier is much cheaper" are examples of such objections. Potential showstoppers, by their very nature, will come back and bite you sooner or later. You may be able to ignore the objections now, but if you do you are just moving a serious objection into the closing phase of a call, where it will be even more difficult to handle. Such objections should in general be handled when they come up.

False objections are objections that the customer gives just to put up a show of resistance. No one wants to just roll over and wave his credit card in the air, even for the best of sellers. Most customers feel they at least need to make some effort to seem hard to get. "I'm a little busy right now," "We're not really looking for a new printer supplier," "I need to think about it" are examples of common "theatrical objections." More often than not, these indicate no other objection than a general objection to your being a seller. Such objections can be serious in themselves, but if you do get away with ignoring them and just pressing on (and often you will) it is unlikely they will come back and bite you later. If the customer accepts that you ignore him when he says "I'm a little busy now," it is unlikely he will repeat that objection when you ask for a credit card 10 minutes later (though he may obviously have other objections).

Buying signals are basically any signs or indications, verbal or nonverbal, that tell you that the lead is (probably) ready to commit to buying. Listening for buying signals is important because those are little openings for you to enter the closing phase. Here is an example of a sale being lost because the seller could not hear clear buying signals. It's based on an actual call I overheard just a few weeks back (the seller was cold calling to sell a phone subscription):

SELLER: OK, John. What we can basically offer is one of the lowest calling rates in the country. We have different plans that suit different call patterns. Tell me a little bit about how you use your phone today. Do you call a lot internationally?

CUSTOMER: No, not really. Just a few times per year.

SELLER: Ah, great! So it's mostly national calls then. Would you say you call more to mobile phones than landlines?

CUSTOMER: These days it's almost all to mobiles, I guess. Um, I hate to interrupt you, but you really need to know I have already decided to change my phone supplier…

SELLER: Oh, I'm sorry to hear that. May I ask whom you decided to go with?

CUSTOMER: Yeah, well, I'm moving to Telephonia4U.

SELLER: Oh. Did they give you a good deal, then?

CUSTOMER: No, not really. It's just a well-known brand, you know…

SELLER: OK, well thanks anyway. And if you change your mind give us a call!

So what happened here? The seller immediately interpreted the phrase "You really need to know I have already decided to change my phone supplier" as an objection rather than a buying signal. This can easily happen when you're cold calling on an autodialer. If you don't keep your focus up, you simply get so used to people cutting you off that you don't even hear it when a customer is begging for the product. You must listen actively and constantly interpret the signals from the customer. Here, instead of seeing this as a perfect opening to move on to closing with "Ah! Good thing I called you today then," the seller completely missed the first buying signal ("I have decided to change my supplier") and then seconds later missed the second buying signal ("No they didn't give me a good deal"). To the unfocused seller this simply didn't register as something positive. He probably did 40 calls in a row where the leads said "no" in one way or another, and at this point his focus was on anything but the potential customer. As chance would have it, one of the managers was listening in on this particular call. In addition to explaining to the seller that he was so useless the kindest thing to do would be to put him to sleep—a move that in the manager's opinion would not greatly influence his performance in the office—the manager told another seller to call the customer back immediately. He closed a deal within minutes.

This is an extreme example, but it illustrates well the dangers of not listening properly to the lead. When you sell, you should remain an active listener. You should not just hear what the potential customer is saying, but also try to work out what he means. The point is to attempt to understand the complete message being sent.

When you hear a buying signal, you need to not only make a mental note of it, but also confirm it back to the client. It makes the buying signal more important to the customer to himself. The call above should have gone something like this:

> *CUSTOMER: These days it's almost all to mobiles, I guess. Um, I hate to interrupt you, but you really need to know I have already decided to change my phone supplier...*
>
> *SELLER: Oh, good thing I called you today then! We'll help you find the best subscription for you and your needs. But first I need a little bit of information about your phone usage. How often do you make international calls?*

We take the buying signal and latch on to it. We used it to advance the call as much as possible to our advantage.

In your sales calls you will probably come across something I refer to as **unconscious buying signals**. Basically the customer is giving you one or more really clear reasons why he should buy your product, but without realizing it himself. Let's say you're selling car insurance and your offer includes a free roadside assistance offer. A potential customer looking for cheap car insurance calls in and during the call he mentions in passing that his car is in the garage for a week and that he has been having problems with that car for months. He may have no idea that you offer complimentary roadside assistance, but he just gave you a fantastic piece of information. What you need to do is to turn that unconscious buying signal into a conscious one. The best way of doing this is by actually making it seem like the customer already had all the information and deliberately decided to call you just for this reason: "Well, Barry, as you know our Gold Comprehensive Cover Plan offers a free roadside assistance service so I guess that is the plan you have been looking at. And to be honest, from what you have told me, I agree with you that this is definitely the best plan for you." You have lifted the accidental information into a proper buying signal, you have lined up for a quick close by selecting the product he is buying, and you have even managed to present it as the customer's own choice!

QUESTIONS FOR THE CLOSING PHASE

As soon as you interpret what the customer is saying as a buying signal, you should change from pitching your product to actually closing the deal. Sadly many sellers don't—either because they don't hear the buying signals or because they are so focused on their own pitch or product that they are unable to stop talking about what they are selling.

> *A few years back I was coaching a very good, but also very young, voiceover talent – teaching him how to actively sell his services to the advertising industry. We had been writing some pitch scripts for him and had identified some good selling points: he had previous experience in radio broadcast, a voice that captured listeners, and his own studio so he could deliver recordings very fast. He had spent some time practicing his pitch and also practicing leading the conversation forward through his pitch by actively asking questions. He now felt ready to start calling. I was listening to the conversation on another line and after not getting past the gatekeepers on his first few calls, he finally got to speak to a project manager at a medium-sized advertising agency. About two minutes into the call, this happened:*

VOICEOVER TALENT: …and one of the things I can offer is my own studio and the ability to supply voiceovers according to scripts within days— sometimes even hours. I presume sometimes you have jobs where there are quite short deadlines?

MANAGER: Well, we do usually plan so as to leave us with comfortable deadlines for all parties, but of course sometimes things come up that we cannot control. Today, for example, the voiceover file for one of our TV advertisements turned out to be corrupt and the voiceover actor is not available to do a new recording this week, so the whole project is being held up…

VOICEOVER TALENT: Yes, I see. I am able to supply all types of file formats of course. What file formats do you usually work with?"

This is enough to make even the most hardened sales coach despair. Here was a potential customer literally saying he was stuck—a whole project delayed—because he couldn't get a voiceover actor to redo a failed recording this week. And the voiceover talent calling to sell himself simply moved on through his own pitch, asking about file formats! Another three minutes into the call, the project manager politely agreed to take down his contact details and let him know if something should come up in the future. A voiceover talent called someone who was desperately in need of an urgent voiceover, and because he wasn't listening for buying signals, they couldn't reach an agreement! It sounds absurd, but this happens all the time—even in the most professional salesrooms. What the voiceover talent should have done, of course, was to immediately register the buying signal, throw his sales pitch out the window and go straight for the close:

"Really? Well it is very fortunate that I called then! Look, what I'll do, since you're in a bit of a spot, is to run home to my studio, do a few recordings and get them over to you to listen to. Since we haven't worked together before, I'll do it free of charge and you only pay me if you use the recording. Does that sound OK? If you email me the script now, I'll get right on it."

Even if in the end they decided not to use him for this project, it would have gotten recordings over to them that they were guaranteed to listen to—and with the quality of this guy's voiceovers, he would have had regular jobs from this agency within weeks.

Some buying signals are too small for you to go directly to closing. But write them down. These are the little convincers that you will use when you are ready to go for the close.

 If you are unsure about the buying signals you are hearing and don't find it safe to move on to a direct closing, you can try a technique known as "trial closing." With this technique you basically ask a question based on the presumption that the lead is buying, but at the same time the question is open enough to give you some room to maneuver if it turns out you are moving too fast. They range from fairly non-committal like "So, John, you can see how the Super Printer 1X can increase efficiency and lower your operating costs, right?" to very blunt questions like "Our printers come in white and bright pink. Which one would you say is the best option for your office landscape?"

There is a nonsense theory floating around online and in a good number of books on sales technique that you need to ask eight trial close questions and get eight "yes" answers from the client before you go for the real close. Many books mention that this has been "statistically proven" yet fail to mention what statistics are supposed to prove this. If one wants to pretend to be scientific, then at least one should pretend to quote a source. As far as I am concerned it is more of the nonsense lifestyle coaches and self-appointed sales gurus have been feeding the world since 1936 (when Dale Carnegie published "How to Win Friends and Influence People"). Of course you don't need to ask eight trial close questions, and of course you don't need eight "yes" responses from the lead before going for a real close. Magic is not a big part of good selling.

However, you do need eight "yes" responses from the customer if you actually ask eight trial close questions. A "no" from the client is obviously not a good thing here.

What you want to do is work on your sales script and pitch so that your trial close questions lead gently into an order form. If John is ordering printers from you, he obviously must provide you with his address, company details, the color of the printers he wants to order and so on and so forth. Unless you are 100% sure the lead is ready to scream "Gimmie, gimmie, gimmie now" then don't start your closing phase by asking "So, you wanna buy or not?" Simply start processing the order. When you feel pretty certain the lead is interested in buying, start tying him down by phrases that confirm the order, such as "OK, John, what I'll do is give a quick call to the warehouse, just to make sure these items are all in stock so I can get them out to you by Friday."

Just to illustrate the process:

SELLER: (…) Do you print a lot of internal papers too, like drafts and notes?

CUSTOMER: Well, yes, I think both finance and admin print a lot of internal documents. And I guess the sellers print a lot of customer data just because they like to work with physical paper when they're on the phone.

SELLER: OK, that's perfect. Our XYZ Super Fine laser printers allow you to set a draft mode, which automatically prints in duplex—on both sides of the sheet—so when we get these printers installed for you, you'll see significant savings on paper usage. Tell me, for letterheads, do you have a standard pre-printed letterhead?

CUSTOMER: Yes, and we have continuation sheets just with a logo too.

SELLER: OK, what I'll do for you is to make sure our IT guys set up the printers to work with these so that the first page is pulled from the letterhead tray and the second page is pulled from the continuation sheet tray.

*By the way, the Hill Street postal address I see here, is
that where you guys have your physical office?*

CUSTOMER: *Yes, it is.*

SELLER: *Cool, so I'll put in 17 Hill Street as a delivery
address then. The XYZ Super Fine is delivered in
off-white as standard. Do you have any special color
requirements?*

CUSTOMER: *Um, no, I don't think so.*

SELLER: *Cool. OK, what I'll do now is give a quick call
to our warehouse to check about delivery time. I think
we have units ready to be shipped, so I don't expect
any problems, but better to make sure. Just hold the
line one second (…) Hello? OK, no problem there. I
have reserved the 25 units and asked the IT guys there
to set them up for letterhead and continuation sheets.
I just need to take down a main phone number for
you guys. I think the 555-7509 I have is your direct
number. What's your main number, is it the 555-7500 I
see here on your home page?*

CUSTOMER: *Yes, um, I…*

SELLER: *OK, cool. Then I have what I need. So the units
are reserved for you guys and being programmed as
we speak. What I'll do now is email you an order
confirmation and what I need you to do is print that
out, sign it and return it by fax or email. Your email
was john@doe-limit.com, right?*

This call illustrates well how the seller throughout the
information phase uses phrases that presume that the
customer is going to buy, like "When we get these printers
installed for you" and "Make sure our IT guys set up the
printers to work with your letterheads" and so on. This
affects how the seller mentally behaves though the call
(giving him increased confidence and keeping him focused
on selling, not informing) and it affects gradually how the
lead thinks. As such phases are repeated again and again
the lead eventually subconsciously accepts that he is buying.

Then the seller moves from information to closing unnoticed. The distinction is there, because now the questions are about delivery and terms, transition is very smooth and subtle. Unless John on some level or other wants to buy (or at least is willing to buy), you can feel pretty confident John at one point nevertheless is going to say "Whoa. Hold your horses there, boy." So we are not talking about tricking the customer here. We are simply using the trial close results to presume that he is buying and to prepare the order. The good thing about this technique is that it changes the premise of the whole sales call. It is no longer your job to convince John to buy, but John's job to convince you he doesn't want to buy. John must actively take some steps to stop the conversation escalating into a sale. To use the terminology from a previous chapter: You have gotten inside his Boyd Loop.

In many situations you do need a final validation of the order, a final "go" from your customer. Sometimes it can be a recording of an order confirmation, sometimes a credit card or a faxed order sheet. But if you use the technique above properly, you will very rarely experience any problems here. Every question on your order form has been like a trial close. It has not only tied John down morally to a degree where he will now look a complete idiot if he doesn't buy (I mean, who discusses delivery dates and colors of a product they don't want to buy?), but most likely John at this point has reconciled himself with the fact that he is buying your product, and hopefully also feels it was both his idea and his decision.

So, if you get a positive reply to your trial close question, don't hesitate. Don't ask seven more trial close questions. Go for your closing pitch. Start taking down the order immediately. I cannot stress this enough. Do not beat about the bush in such situations. The customer has indicated he will buy, so go for it. People's moods change constantly and just because a lead is hot and read to go for it now, doesn't mean he will be so in one, three or five minutes from now. When you have your clear buying signals, it's time to close the deal. No more product information and chitchat.

From here on we talk only about *how* the customer is going to order. When does he want the printers delivered? How many printers does he want? Which model does he want? Will he pay by cash, check or credit card? You may want to reword the questions slightly, but this is what we talk about now: it's all about "how," not "if." And as I mentioned in page 55, once we have crossed the line into closing, we must not, cannot ever go back to the information phase again.

It is usually a good idea to take a close look at your order form (if your company uses a standard one) and analyze each question on it. You want to organize the form questions from easy to hard, in the sense of information hard to obtain from the customer. Questions that are normally easy to get an answer to are obvious, such as email, postal address, and phone number. You want to ask them in a matter-of-fact way: "Could I just make a note of your email address, please?" "By the way, John, what's the best phone number to reach you?" and so on and so forth.

From there we move on to a middle level of questions. These are still fairly standard questions, but they make it more obvious to the customer that she is committing to buying. Here we find questions like delivery address, which model the customer prefers and so on. Again we want to make sure we use a matter-of-fact way of asking them, making the questions part of the natural flow of the conversation. But at the same time we also want to be communicating more clearly that as far as we are concerned, the customer is now in the process of placing the order. So we want to sneak in remarks that make this clear, such as "When we deliver the printers…" "When you start using these copiers…":

"When we deliver the printers to you, I'll also make sure we give you 20 extra user manuals so you can distribute these to your employees. By the way, John, which color would you guys prefer? Would you say the white or black model would fit best into your current office landscape?"

Or

"When we have installed the copiers in your office, what I'll make sure we do is to have one of our guys come over there and train a few of your key employees so that you have someone in the office who knows all the features and can assist the rest of the staff when they start using the printers. By the way, John, could I just make a note of your delivery address? What is the physical address of your office?"

Finally we move toward the "closing proper" questions. These are the ones where there really cannot be any doubt that an order is being placed. This can be asking for a credit card or asking the customer to fax back a copy of an order form. Here we want to be much more direct. We have now spent the last few minutes at least constantly making it clear that we are taking down an order, but we have kept the conversation flowing so it has been difficult for the customer to actually say "Hold up. Are you taking down an order?" The customer knows this and it helps to tie him down. He will probably at this stage feel that he has led you to believe that he is placing an order. Why would anyone confirm their delivery address or the color of models to be delivered if they don't want to place an order? People do not like to disappoint nor do they like to look like idiots.

Now we can actively use that pressure the customer feels in this situation by being very direct and combine it with such techniques as "silent closing" (see page 106).

Some of the best sellers prefer to do a little prelude before their final, real closing questions. This is a short speech that is prewritten and well-rehearsed by the seller so that pace and timing is perfect. In the prelude we make it sure that we stress even further that this is an order and tell the customer what is going to happen:

SELLLER: OK, Justin, I now have the information I need. So what I'll do now is to send this up to Finance for a final approval and then I'll give you a call to confirm. Do you have pen and paper there?

CUSTOMER: Um, yes?

SELLER: Great, make a note of my name and direct phone number in case you have any questions. My name is Chris Cross and you can reach me on 555-1234. OK, so I'll give you a call tomorrow just to confirm. My morning is a bit busy with some meetings but I have most of the afternoon free. When would suit you best, 4 PM or 6 PM?

CUSTOMER: Um, I'm in the office until 5…

SELLER: OK, perfect. I'll call you at about 4:30 then. Now, I just need you to confirm your order. We do this on the phone, and that part of the call is recorded. I'll ask you a few questions and you just need to answer "Yes," OK. So here we go. Today is January 1, 2015, and I'm talking to Justin Case from Justin Case You need Tools Inc. Correct? (…)

Instead of a confirmation recording you could ask for a credit card number or instruct him to return a signed order form by fax in more or less the same manner. The whole point in this regard is the call structure. We start by gradually mentally tying the customer down by light questions that he answers without much thinking, such as his full name or his email address. Then we move on to slightly more complicated questions like what model he prefers. We keep the conversation flowing naturally and throw in little hints that we are considering this an order, just to tie him down even more. Then we change the style and become formal. Now we are confirming an order that, although the customer will have seen was coming, the transition has been so smooth that he never really has one clear point at which to say "Hold on a second; I need to think about this for a day."

This is an extremely efficient way of closing because we subconsciously change the dynamics of the sales from our convincing the client to say "Yes" to the client having to say "No."

INTERRUPTIONS

Handling interruptions on the phone can be quite tricky. Unlike a face-to-face meeting you have no visual clues to when a person is trying to get a word in. Nor can you use such clues, like leaning forward, raising your hands or in any other way visually signal that you really want to say something. For this reason, interruptions on the phone usually come suddenly and unexpectedly and can often seem rude.

Interruptions obviously can go both ways: You may be interrupting the customer or the customer may be interrupting you. There is one golden rule if a customer interrupts you on the phone, and that is to *not* stop talking. Psychologically the one who is allowed to interrupt is in charge of the conversation. And you definitely don't want the lead to be in charge. You want to make sure you control the call from opening to close.

This doesn't mean you have to be rude. In most cases the interruption is simply a single syllable uttered by the lead before he realizes you are talking. Accidental interruptions on the phone are in fact quite common, due to the lack of visual signals. Perhaps you thought the lead was done talking and started talking yourself, or perhaps the lead thought you were done talking while you were in fact just pausing for effect. Whatever the case may be, keeping talking is in general the best option here because you stay in control of the call. If you stop talking it will also often lead to an even more confused and uncomfortable situation for both parties because in general the lead will realize he has interrupted you and stop talking himself, before both people start talking again at the same time. Nothing can ruin the flow of the call more than 15 seconds of "You," "No, you, "Sorry, you go ahead," like two people meeting in the street not agreeing on which side to pass.

If you keep talking and the customer does not back down, but instead keeps on talking, you can be pretty sure you are dealing with a tricky lead with a lot of self-confidence and self-belief. Give it a second or two, but then stop talking by simply saying "Hello, hello? The line is really bad. Are you there?" Blaming technical problems gets rid of much of the tension and also stops his flow so you may be lucky and regain some control.

As for the other situations, where you as a seller interrupt the lead, the general rule is simply "Don't." Interrupting a lead is generally not good sales technique. It is a sign that you are not listening actively enough, but rather focusing too much on your own pitch. In addition it is obviously irritating to the lead and you will often come off as overly pushy.

There are, however, some instances where you deliberately may want to interrupt a potential customer. Certain objections can be very difficult to actually solve as a seller. Among such objections are "We are not ready to commit yet," "I just want some information," "Send me a brochure," "I need to think about it" and so on. These objections are of a type I refer to as "false objections," which I will cover in more detail later (page 114). For now it is sufficient to know that these objections by their very nature cannot be handled logically by you as a seller. If the lead is allowed to say these objections out loud, the objection is reinforced in the lead's mind. And since the very nature of the objections makes them impossible for you to solve, such objections tend to come back and haunt you when you move on to the closing. Even if the lead allows you to ignore these objections early on in the call, you run a high risk of getting renewed objections in the closing phase, such as "But I said I only want information" or "Look, I told you already that I need to think about this."

So what we ideally want as a seller is preventing the lead from mentioning the objection in the first place. If you prevent the lead from saying it out loud, he will often forget about it within a few seconds. And if you haven't heard it, the lead cannot play the but-I-told-you card. As sellers we obviously try to avoid these objections by controlling the call well. If you keep asking questions that engage the customer, he simply will not be able to think about such objections and definitely not say them out loud. However, even the best phone sellers lose control of the call from time to time. In such situations, if you listen actively (and with experience and practice), you will often know when the customer is about to raise one of these objections. If you end up in that situation, you really need to do what you can to stop the customer from actually saying it. And the only way you can do this is by interrupting him.

When we interrupt the customer in such a situation, we try to do it politely. And nothing seems more harmless than accidentally talking at the same time as the client. If there is a small pause, just use it to start talking. The lead will probably start talking himself, but when he realizes you are talking, if he is like the majority of people, he will stop. Do not stop yourself.

If there is no pause, simply say "Hello, hello? Are you there?" or something like this to give the impression that you cannot hear the client. Practically any lead will, at this point, answer something like "Yes, I can hear you fine." Take the opportunity to take back control of the call now. Immediately follow up with something like "Oh, sorry, I can hear you fine now. There must have been a problem on my end…we have…Oh, before I forget: you are running a Windows network in your office, right?" By interrupting yourself, like you just remembered something, you haven't sounded pushy or rude. But at the same time you have managed to prevent the objection from being said out loud and you have asked a question that the lead will hopefully now focus on and answer. Then stay very proactive for the next 30 to 60 seconds. Increase the pace slightly and keep asking questions that engage the customer. That way, by the time you get back to your standard pitch, hopefully the customer will have forgotten about his planned objection.

Again, just to avoid any misunderstandings: This relates to a specific type of objection. It's the type of illogical delay tactics of the type "I want a brochure first" or "I just need to think about it" we want to prevent. Other objections we want to handle properly. If you think a customer is about to say that this product is too expensive or the product doesn't match his needs, let him say it and then handle it properly. Such objections are usually good for your sales (you can flip it around and say "OK, but if I can arrange XYZ, I guess we are ready to go, right?), and in any case they are fair objections that should be taken seriously by you as a seller. Selling is not about cheating; it's about connecting a lead to the right product for him and convincing him that that is what you're doing. Unfair delay tactics from the lead, though, present something as immoral as dirty selling. If he doesn't want the product, then he should say so. If he thinks it too expensive, he should say it and maybe you can fix it. "I want to think about it" or "I just want a brochure" are meaningless objections that just keep you working by following up on a lead who either could have bought right away or will never buy because he doesn't like the product but is too weak to say so.

There is another useful tip that I should mention under interruptions. It doesn't relate to the customer's interrupting you or your interrupting the customer, but rather your interrupting yourself. It sounds silly, but interrupting yourself can help you keep control of a call that is heading in the wrong direction or help you transition from one phase of the call to another because the interruption provides a natural bridge to something else:

CUSTOMER: *"Those printers of yours, can they also print in duplex mode?"*

SELLER: *"Yes, Jerry, of course! Our printers can be set to print in duplex as default and..."*

CUSTOMER: *"OK, good. But can they be set individually by the person printing?"*

SELLER: *"Yes, the print driver allows the person printing to select normal or duplex pri... Oh, I almost forgot, Jerry, could I make a note of your email address, just so that I know how to contact you electronically? What is your email address?"*

CUSTOMER: *"Um, sure, it's jerry.atrick@atrickmedical. com"*

In this example the seller realized that he was losing control of the call. The customer was asking questions fast and was beginning to decide the direction of the conversation. It could work out well, but from experience the seller knew that it could also quickly mean that Jerry got to say "Sounds good. Send me a brochure" which would ruin any chances of a quick close. By beginning to answer, but then interrupting himself before the customer got a chance to do so again, the seller managed to take control back and bring the call back to his script. The quick move from one subject to another was sufficient to make Jerry just answer the question as a reflex.

DELIBERATE SILENCE AND PAUSES

Silence or long pauses represent perhaps the opposite of deliberately interrupting a potential customer. But if timed correctly, they can have considerable effect on your sales.

Scientists claim to have identified an interval length referred to as a "human moment." This is a timeframe which seems encoded into all humans by which we measure activity. A human moment defines the longest window that we can perceive as an independent event. A study published in Journal of Ethology, based on among other things, the research of how long humans could hug strangers without feeling uncomfortable, identified a human moment as 3.2 seconds. Basically a hug of one second is perceived as cold and dismissive, while a hug lasting five seconds seems as if you have some other agenda or have accidentally glued yourself to the other person.

This is also true for speech. If you want to pace your speech perfectly, you want to avoid pauses that are so short you sound pushy, yet not so long that they become embarrassing. Again three seconds seem to be the upper limit. If you are silent for more than three seconds, the other person will feel a growing pressure to say something, anything.

As a seller you can use silent pauses to your advantage in two ways. First we have the **silent closing**. This is basically asking a sensitive question and keeping your mouth shut until the customer talks. Though it can be efficient as a technique, sales literature has put too much emphasis on silent closing as a separate closing technique. Let's be honest: it is less an independent closing technique than loose advice to not blabber on after asking a sensitive question. The actual closing is in the job you do up until you ask the question. It is no good asking "So do we have a deal?" and then keeping your mouth shut for the next 20 seconds unless the customer is ready to buy. If, however, you have done your closing well up to this point, asking a question and keeping silent can put additional pressure on the client to answer in the positive. And on the flipside, asking "Do we have a deal?" and then not being quiet, but nervously blabbering on with "...because this is really the best option for you, you know, I mean, um, it's really a good price and you can probably not get a better deal, um, and you will get all these benefits and the free I Love Printer T-shirt" is obviously going to mess up your sale.

In addition to the silent closing, you can use an understanding of the human moment and the three-second rule to control pace and interruptions. If the client is done talking and you want him to keep talking, waiting more than three seconds before you start talking will lead to the customer feeling subconsciously pressured to continue. Let's say your potential customer has explained a little bit about his office printer setup and you want him to give you even more info, instead of saying "Really? Tell me more" you can simply wait more than three seconds before you start talking and more often than not he will start talking on his own. Using this technique can be incredibly efficient. Be aware, however, that it should be used only in the less sensitive parts of your sales calls, when you feel you have good control on the customer and when the customer feels safe and doesn't worry you will try to sell him something right now. If not you run the risk of losing control and the customer saying something like "Um, I'm very busy now; can you call me tomorrow."

Again you can use your knowledge of the three-second rule to achieve the opposite effect too. If you are talking yourself and want to make sure you keep control and continue to talk, keep your pauses well below three seconds. You don't have to talk without any pauses at all, like you've just had 35 cups of coffee and are about to have a nervous breakdown. Just keep your pauses comfortably below three seconds; two seconds or so is usually safe. People will hesitate to start talking until you have been silent for longer than three seconds.

NEVER ARGUE WITH THE LEAD

The two people in the world with the most direct impact on your paycheck as a phone seller are your boss and the customer at the other end of your phone line.

Few people will make a habit of slapping their bosses in the face—and those who do tend to have very limited career prospects. Yet it remains a constant source of amazement and frustration to me that I keep hearing phone sellers getting into arguments with their potential customers.

In this book I keep referring to how you need to stay in charge of the call in order to maximize your chances of a sale. The potential customer, though, will always remain in ultimate charge of his wallet. Whether you need a signed contract, a confirmation on the phone or the sixteen digits from his credit card; at the end of the day, your potential customer is your key to closing the sale. If he hangs up or tells you to get lost, you're not going to make any money. If you learn only one sales technique from this book, it should be this one: Never, never, never argue with a person to whom you are trying to sell something.

If you want to convince someone to buy something from you or enter into a project with you—or even just employ you—arguing in a negative way is never going to get you anywhere. And by arguing I mean any sort of immediate and clear contradiction. Using words or phrases like "but," "I am not sure if I totally agree with you there," or "that is perhaps not entirely correct" are big no-nos. It doesn't matter what the lead says. If he says, "Your company doesn't have the experience we are looking for," your immediate reaction will be to say "but..." and give some argument for why this is not correct. Don't! How often have you had an argument with someone and within a few minutes she has said, "You're right! I've been a complete idiot. What you have been saying all along makes sense now." It just doesn't happen. The other person is the key to whatever you want to achieve (basically a sale). You don't want him or her to be in a negative mood; you want the conversation always to remain positive. If someone says, "Your company doesn't have the experience we are looking for," the right way to respond is to say something to make him feel he was right, but still give an argument to buy from you: "I fully understand your concerns; your company's requirements are obviously unique. I do believe, however, our wide experience from XYZ would prove very valuable for the job, particularly our experience with Linux networks. Your current printer network, I understand, is Linux-based, right?" It may not convince the customer, but it certainly gives you a better chance than saying, "I think you are wrong about this."

Whatever the customer says, your reply should start as a positive. Your sentence should begin with "certainly," "I fully understand," "of course" or any similar positive worded phrase to confirm that you're definitely on the customer's team. It doesn't matter what the customer said; you always reply positively. Then of course after having confirmed that you're definitely on the customer's side, you may want to say whatever you need to say to steer the conversation toward a sale. But you do it playing with the customer, not playing against the customer.

The customer says he wants to think about this? Oh, not good! But do you reply with "Why on earth do you need to think about it; you already thought about it for three weeks"? Of course not. You're not an idiot. You start your reply with "I fully understand" and then you tell him in a positive way that although you fully understand that he wants to wait, what we'll do is to just close the deal now:

> CUSTOMER: *"Look, John. I haven't had time to read all the material you sent over. I need to think about this."*
>
> SELLER: *"Certainly, Barry! I fully understand. What we'll do is that I'll complete the order form, and then I'll give you a call tomorrow and we can go through everything. But let me just take down your delivery address. What's the physical location of your office?"*

That sounds a bit more likely to result in a sale, doesn't it, than:

> CUSTOMER: *"Look, John. I haven't had time to read all the material you sent over. I need to think about this."*
>
> SELLER: *"Why do you need to think this over? I mean, I sent you all the details weeks ago."*

The trick is to reply positively, even to something negative from the customer, and then still say what you want to say while making it sound like you are complying with the customer's request. And as always, end with a question to divert attention away and regain control of the call.

Another example:

> CUSTOMER: *"Look John, I really think we are moving a bit too fast here. I'm not ready to commit yet."*
>
> SELLER: *"Sure, Barry. I fully understand. I apologize if I seemed overly excited. Since we both agreed these printers are something that will definitely save you both time and money, I was just anxious to get you*

> *guys up and running. What I'll do is to take down the order, but before I send anything off for fulfillment I'll come up to your office with a few printers and you can make sure you see exactly how good they are and that they will suit your needs. Are you in the office tomorrow afternoon?*

Again the technique is the same. Agree with the customer, then say what you want to say in a way that sounds like you did what the customer wanted you to do. And then divert attention with a new question.

Sometimes, particularly if you've moved too quickly into the closing phase, the customer may actually notice that what you really did was to ignore his objections in a very roundabout way. But if you have kept your voice friendly and accommodating, he will rarely be upset. If Barry in the above example repeated something like "No, John, I really need to think about this," then just play the same strategy again, but back a little bit further down: "Oh, OK. Sure Barry! I'm going to put your order process on hold then, so it is here to be completed when you are ready to proceed. Meanwhile, though, I'd really like for you to see the printers in action in your office. When would it be convenient for you to have me drop by your office with some demo models?"

As long as you remain positive and sound cheerful, customers generally do not become angry. So you have very little to lose on this strategy. And it gives you a few extra shots at getting a close. You'll be surprised how efficient it is. It is certainly better than arguing with the customer. (In fact, so is hanging up the phone. At least then you can call back later and blame it on technical difficulties.)

"No, Sir, according to my script you are now supposed to ask for the price".

HANDLING OBJECTIONS

The author and motivational speaker Zig Ziglar apparently said, "Every sale has five basic obstacles: no need, no hurry, no desire, no trust, no money." And basically any objection you will encounter in a sales call will fit into one of these categories. As a seller, then, what you must do is to create need, generate urgency, build desire, encourage trust and ask if the customer can borrow a credit card from a friend. Ideally you will offer all this to the customer before he can even raise the issues himself. But in every sale the potential customer will have some sort of objection, one or more reasons for not buying. It's your job to make sure he forgets about them.

The most important aspect of handling objections is to realize that they are a natural phase of any sale. This is simply how things work. If people just wanted your product on their own, if they didn't need any convincing, the world wouldn't need sellers.

As I have previously briefly touched upon, there are basically two fundamentally different types of objections from your potential client during the sales process: false objections and proper objections.

False objections are either just delay tactics by the potential client or simply "stuff we say when a seller calls." Because many people, especially decision-makers in businesses, are so used to being called by sellers, many have developed a set of standard objections that they present without either thinking or listening. Here are some standard false objections:

"I just wanted a brochure."

No one just wants a brochure unless he is trying to build a collection of some sort. Think about it. Why would anyone just want the brochure? It's insane. People may want a brochure, but that is surely not all they want. If you ask for a brochure you must have a basic interest in the product covered by the brochure. And what is even better than a brochure? A seller who knows the products in and out and can answer all your questions, not just the standard sales pitch of a brochure!

"Call me tomorrow/next week."

Really? What will have changed by tomorrow or next week? Unless this is preceded by an explanation of why the situation will be totally different then, this is just nonsense and a waste of the seller's time and the lead's time.

"I must think about it."

No! No one must just think about "it." If I as a seller have just presented you with all the facts you need, if you have all the relevant information, then you are in a position to make a decision now. You will be neither more nor less in a position to make a decision next month. And let's be honest, it is not like we are going to hang up now, and you will go into your office, close the door and spend the next 30 days in deep contemplation about my offer's pros and cons. On the contrary, when I call you in a month from now your response will be "Oh, yes, um. You were the guy with the cheap printers, right?" and we will be exactly where we are now except you will still have crummy printers and I will be a month older. If you are going to think about it, tell me what you are going to think about. Are you comparing my offer with someone else's? Fine, but tell me about it and maybe we can do something about the price. Are you going to check with your IT guys to see if our printers will work on your network? Sure, go ahead, but keep me on the line because you're probably going to need some information. Thinking about the elusive "it" on the other hand, is just pointless.

"I'm a little busy right now. Can you call me later?"

Of course you are busy right now. You are working —and so am I. I'm working trying to sell printers to you. But will calling you "later" really help? When is "later" anyway, and if I do figure out when it is, is it likely that you will then in anxious expectation have shut down your email reader, turned off your phone and closed the door to your office, sitting, staring at the wall, excitedly thinking "When is he going to call?" Any phone seller knows that "Call me later" is merely a reflex, something said by the lead without the brain ever being involved, like the kicking reflex when hit on the knee or pulling your hand away if you accidentally put it on a hot plate. When I call you later you will be equally busy and we'll both just be a little older. "I'm in a meeting now; can you call in an hour?" is of course different. Notice the distinction here: "I'm in a meeting right now" offers a proper explanation for why this is an inconvenient time and a fairly exact time frame for a callback. (Unless you're calling a cardinal during a conclave, the meeting is unlikely to last days) Unlike being just busy in general, being in a meeting is not a false objection.

False objections tend to come in two phases of the sales call. Most of them come within a few seconds of the opening of the call, and are true reflex by the potential customer. You could have called and said, "Hi, my name is Bill Gates and I'm giving away a million dollars," and he still would have replied, "I'm a little busy now." The other phase when you will encounter false objections is the beginning of the closing phase, when you move on to actually confirm the order. Here the false objections are less of a reflex and more of a panic reaction by customers too afraid to commit and too weak to say "No."

Since these false objections are not rooted in anything material that you can handle or fix as a seller, you really have just one option and that is to ignore them. You can either pretend that you never heard what the lead said or you can use a technique often referred to as the "quick question technique." The latter is normally the least risky and the best to use in the opening phase. It works by basically saying "Sure! Can I just ask you a few quick questions?" and then ask a question without waiting for a reply:

CUSTOMER: *"Um, I'm a little busy right now. Can you call me tomorrow?"*

SELLER: *"Sure! If I can just ask a few quick questions. Your current printing setup, is it network based or desktop based?"*

People don't like to interrupt and as I have mentioned, people tend to focus on questions asked them and forget what they were talking about themselves. Just keep the conversation flowing for a while with some more quick questions and then move on to the information phase, for example by saying something like "Ah! Then it's a good thing I called you. What I can help you with…" or "Ah! Now I really understand why you are interested in our Photo Kopy X1! What I can help you with…" or words to that effect.

False objections in the closing phase can be a little more sensitive. What you need to understand is that false objections here, as I mentioned, are nearly always caused by a commitment fear by the customer. These are people who are inherently disposed to wanting to delay any decision as long as possible—preferably indefinitely. It doesn't mean they are not interested in the product.

> *This is equally bad for both you as a seller and for the potential customer. Because you keep calling these leads back, both parties waste time that most probably could have been much better spent. Statistically very few of these people actually ever get around to making the decision. Unless there is some real, tangible reason for the customer to delay committing, there is no reason to think that the next call is going to be any different.*

The way to handle false objections in the closing phase is basically to reduce the perceived risk exposure by the potential customer. This way you address the actual problem: the customer's fear of committing to a deal, rather than the perceived problem (the customer "being busy," "having to think about it" and so on).

You can do this by using the "I'll be there for you all the way" tactic. This is to give the customer a feeling of security by knowing that you will not just take his money and escape to the Bahamas. Here is an example:

SELLER: OK, Jane. So what I'll do is to put that order through for you. Just hold the line while I call the

*warehouse and confirm that we can deliver by
Monday.*
CUSTOMER: *Yeah, um, well. I mean I really need to
think about this…*
SELLER: *Absolutely, Jane. What I'll do is to put that
order through and then I'll call you Monday when you
have received the printers and then we'll go through
the entire installation process and make sure this is
exactly what you need for your office and make sure we
make any amendments to the order if it is not a perfect
match for you, OK? Just hold the line while I confirm
that we can deliver on Monday.*

Because the seller here understands that Jane doesn't really
want to go into deep contemplation about an elusive "it"
but is just panicking a little because she is about to commit
to buying 550 new laser network printers for her office, the
seller responds not to what Jane said, but to what Jane meant.
By assuring Jane that she won't be alone on Monday, and by
assuring Jane that these printers are going to be perfect for
her, and if they aren't by any odd chance, then we'll amend
the order to make sure they will be, then Jane can calm down
enough to allow the order to go through.

Another technique that a lot of sellers use in this phase is
to start talking directly about guarantees and cooling-off
periods. I don't like this at all. The flip side of a guarantee
is that something breaks and the flip side of a cooling-off
period is that the customer has just made a rash and stupid
decision. So when a lead says "I don't know. I really need to
think about this" and the seller replies "Don't worry, John,
you have a 14-day cooling-off period so you can change your
mind and return the products" he is really just underlining
the fact that John is about to make a rash decision. In my
opinion this tends to make John more, not less, nervous.

The most hopeless of excuses from the potential customer in the closing phase is the "I'm a little busy now. Can we do this tomorrow?" excuse. Unlike when used in the opening phase, the lead will usually immediately hear for himself how ridiculous this excuse is when used in the closing phase. Most likely the potential customer has already spent 10, 15 or 30 minutes on the phone with you without mentioning that he is too busy, so why on earth would he be too busy to spend another 30 seconds to confirm the order. As a seller you can handle this objection like any other objection in the closing phase, by assuring him indirectly that this is a safe choice. It most likely originates from the customer's same commitment fear as the more intelligent objections. But because the lead will usually himself hear how feeble his excuse is, it (as possibly the only of the false objections in the closing phase) can usually be dismissed simply by "Sure, John, I understand. This will take only a minute. So what time on Monday is best for you for delivery? Noon or 4 PM?"

Like "the dog ate my homework excuse" at school, false objections, particularly in the closing phase, luckily have an upper usage limit of one. If your homework is regularly eaten by your dog at school, you'll start to look more stupid than unlucky, and if a lead is "too busy right now," has to "think about it" and "just wants a brochure," he too might start to sound, even to himself, a bit silly. But, like most other excuses, as long as you call enough people, you will eventually come across someone who's panic in the closing phase is so complete that he will pour out any feeble excuse he can think of. Let's be honest; someone who does this rather than taking a proper stand and saying "No" is an extremely weak person. My favorite technique of handling these leads, therefore, is to simply ask straight out "John, you do want these printers, right?" Because the lead has spent 10, 15 or 30 minutes on the phone with you, because he has been too weak to say "No" and because he knows all this very well himself, practically without fail these leads will answer something like "Yes, of course! It's just that, um, I…" Simply follow up by saying something like "John, I fully understand. But you want these printers and I want to sell them to you because I know they are what you need for your office. So what I'll do is to confirm your order now, OK, and then I'll put you on hold for just a second while I check with our warehouse to make sure we can deliver on Monday. OK, John?" Like well-trained puppies, almost without fail, they will say "Yes. OK."

> *Again a little reminder here because I know how the last paragraph might sound: good selling is not about cheating. It's about connecting people with products that are good for them. A lot of people out there have a basic commitment fear, even when presented with products they clearly need or products they will clearly benefit from. Their fears of actually committing to a deal often prevent them from growing their business and leave them with outdated systems or technical equipment. As sellers it is our job to make sure these customers are forced to make deliberate decisions. They don't have to buy, but they should say "yes" or "no." These people tend to prefer "maybe" and that is not helping them, nor is it helping us. Don't get me wrong here: Good selling is definitely not about finding weak people and then pushing them to buy poor products they don't need. Today consumer protection regulations and the reputation risk posed by the Internet make such sales strategies extremely short-sighted. The good thing about selling on the phone is that there is usually always another number to call. And if you come across a potential customer who clearly doesn't need your product, there is no reason today to waste your time trying to sell him something and risk your and your company's reputation by pushing him into a deal that is not good for him. Good selling sometimes involves hanging up and calling the next lead.*

 As I mentioned above, most false objections come in the beginning of your calls or toward the closing. If you start getting a lot of false objections in the middle of your call, it's time to take a serious look at your pitch. Most likely it is long-winded and plain boring: You talk too much, listen too little and simply do not engage the potential customer. When he says, "Look, I'm a little busy right now," in the middle of your call, he is probably just bored stiff and wants to get rid of you. Revise your pitch to be more customer-focused. Make the customer talk about himself and he will never be bored.

Unlike false objections, **proper objections** are objections that you as a seller can handle logically. You may or may not be able to solve the objection, but it is an objection that deserves attention and must be handled before proceeding with the sale.

Because you must use your logic and sales technique to actually solve proper objections, it is extremely important that you focus on what the potential customer is saying. Listen intently and allow the customer to finish completely before you start talking. The objection is a proper one and disserves your attention, and it is important to let your customer know you take him serious.

> *Again remember the three-second rule I discussed earlier. After the customer has finished talking, allow at least two to three seconds before you start replying. This underlines the fact that you are listening and thinking about what the customer has just told you.*

Proper objections generally fall in two categories: objections relating to your product or service and objections relating to price and terms.

Both types of objections, as I have touched upon earlier, are in general good. They indicate a basic interest in your product. The potential customer is basically saying "I want to buy, but…" You can therefore successfully use the objections to close a sale. If you solve the problem to the customer's satisfaction, he has more or less already said he is ready to buy.

Objections on price or terms are generally loved by sellers. They are extremely clear because their scope is so limited.

If you can meet the customer's expectations, a sale is almost assured.

Other objections must obviously be handled on a case-to-case basis. After the potential customer has explained his concerns, to which you have listened carefully and intently, analyze the objection. Make sure you fully understand exactly what the customer is concerned about. This means not just understanding what the customer said, but also what the customer meant. Most of the time this will obviously be the same thing. But some customers tend to shy away from objections that they fear may be insulting. You can usually spot this by the customer being very general when attempting to describe his concern, such as "We prefer to work with bigger companies" or "We only work with companies here in Milwaukee." It doesn't take much analytical skill to deduce that the customer most likely isn't actually concerned about the size of your company or location of your office as such—it really makes no difference to him whether you're a sole trader operating out of your own bedroom or a huge multinational corporation with thousands of employees. What he is probably concerned about is support and general after-sales service, product quality and so on. The customer is presuming that a bigger company will have better customer service or presuming that it will be easier to handle a problem with a company just down the road. You handle these objections by analyzing and understanding the root of the customer's concern and using logical arguments to handle the real objections. Ten employees offering great after-sale support would normally be better for the customer than 10,000 on a bad, outsourced helpline in India, for example. If you provide proper explanation, you will be able to put such concerns at rest and move on with your sales.

 Because it is extremely important to understand exactly what the customer's concern is in order for you to be able to handle the objection properly, you need to take great care when analyzing what the customer is saying. If you are ever in doubt, ask more questions. Then, when you know the exact concern of the customer, address it and nothing else. From the example above:

CUSTOMER: "Well, we prefer to work with bigger companies…"

SELLER: "I fully understand that, John. Am I right in presuming this is because in general you might be concerned smaller companies are not able to offer the same level of after-sale support?"

CUSTOMER: "Yes, well, we have had some bad experiences lately…"

SELLER: "OK, I understand, John. This seems to be the last stumbling block for us to do business together, so I'll tell you what I'll do: We have a special after-sales service and support plan where we give you a dedicated person here to handle all your needs, and in addition you get a 24/7 emergency line and we guarantee that we will be in your office to take care of any issues or provide replacement printers within three working hours. This is really a plan reserved for government offices and our largest customers, but if you hold the line, I'll call my manager and check to see if we can offer you the same service. OK?"

You have now successfully analyzed the customer's concern, asked questions to make sure you have interpreted the concern correctly and you have come up with a solution and used it to, almost certainly, close a deal.

Whatever approach you use to handle the objection, keep reminding yourself that objections are good because they are an indication of a basic interest in your products.

As in the example above, make sure you actively use the fact that you are solving the objection to tie down the customer as much as possible. Do not just blurt out, "No problem, we'll fix it!" Use the objection to the maximum by stressing the problem, stressing the fact that you understand that this is what is preventing the customer from committing, and then and only then find the solution. Make it sound as something you are actively working to solve, even if this is something you immediately know the solution to. If you are allowed to give a 20% discount and the client is complaining that the price is 15% too high, don't go, "Oh, don't worry, I'll knock off 20%, OK?" Make it sound like it is a bit of work on your end.

CUSTOMER: *"John, I'll be honest with you. I like your printers—they seem ideal for us. But our current supplier is at least 15% cheaper than you guys. I really don't think the extra cost is for us justified by the additional functionality. I mean, the duplex printing function is great, but it's not something we'll be using much."*

SELLER: *"Look, Peter, I fully understand. I'll be honest with you, because, as you say, our printers offer much more functionality than most of our competitors'; it's really hard for us to be competitive on price alone. Um, look, this really seems like a deal-breaker to you guys, and I really want to work with you so you get to see the quality we offer... Let me try to give a call to my boss. I really can't promise anything, and definitely not 15%, but if I were to get you a really good discount, just so I know what to tell my boss, how quickly would you expect delivery? Would next Monday be quick enough?"*

CUSTOMER: *"Yes, I guess so..."*

SELLER: *"OK, Peter. Just hang on one second and I'll see if I can get hold of my boss. The line will go silent but stay on the line, OK?"*

(...)

SELLER: *"Hello, Peter? I got hold of my boss. He wasn't thrilled but I managed to secure you guys a 15%*

> *discount! What I'll do is to give our warehouse a quick*
> *call to reserve the units and make sure we can get them*
> *out to you on Monday. Will between noon and 4 PM*
> *be OK?"*

With that approach the deal is basically done. It is extremely difficult for a potential customer who presented price as the deal-breaker not to agree to the deal when you got him the price he wanted. But what really tied him down was the way you built up the objection into the last obstacle standing between you and him doing business together. If you had just immediately given him a 20% discount, the customer might very easily have come up with more reasons to delay a decision.

Some objections cannot be solved, but you may be able to twist and misunderstand the objection to your advantage. Let's say a potential customer calls in for more information about a family deal on car insurance for him and his wife. The call is going great and you pull him all the way through your script and down to your close. Then suddenly there is a problem:

> *CUSTOMER: "Look, John. This sounds really good but*
> *I don't think I can sign up for new insurance until I*
> *have just spoken quickly with my wife."*
> *SELLER: "Sure, Barry, I understand. No problem at all.*
> *What I'll do then is to set up a cover for your car, at*
> *a family rate, and then when you have spoken to your*
> *wife just give me a call and I'll add her car too. So*
> *your car is the Ford, right?"*

So what happened here? What the customer meant is that he didn't want to sign up for anything until he checked with his wife. But we deliberately didn't understand it in that way.

If we had, we would have had to sit patiently waiting for the lead to talk to his wife. That would have meant losing control of the process and as a seller that is the last thing we want. Instead we decided to spin the objection so that we would just arrange insurance for his car now, and then add the wife's car later. If the customer objects again, we'll of course correct the mistake and back down. But this gave us one more shot at a direct close.

One last technique I want to touch upon relating to objection handling is what I call seller-created objections. Basically **seller-created objections** are objections that the potential customer has neither mentioned nor probably even thought of. It may at first sound absurd that you as a seller would create a reason for the customer not to buy. But think about it: I have shown above how easy it is for a good seller to use an objection to close a sale. If you can create an objection that you can solve, you may be able to move on to closing with a lead who would otherwise have been difficult to get beyond the informational stages.

Seller-created objections can be risky, but when they work, they can be great tools for you as a seller. They are particularly useful in three instances: handling false objections, planning for callbacks and moving difficult leads from information to closing.

As a tool for handling false objections, seller-created objections work simply by your interpreting the false objection in a way that suits you, but may not have occurred to the potential customer at all:

CUSTOMER: "Look, Jane, I really need to think about this."

SELLER: "OK, Pam, I understand. I guess your main concern is the lack of networking features on our printers, right? I mean, the way you guys have set up your office infrastructure, I can see how this may be a big problem for you…"

CUSTOMER: "Um, yes, it is really, um, difficult for us to work with someone who doesn't offer network printing as standard."

SELLER: "Look, Pam, I really want to work with you guys. As you see yourself, our prices are way below what you are paying today. And it is really frustrating that the lack of network integration is the only thing preventing a deal. Um, look, it's a wild shot, but let me give IT a call to see if there is anything they can do about this. I don't hold much hope, but I guess it's worth a shot. Just so I know when I talk to them, how quickly do you need the new printers? Would Monday two weeks from now be soon enough?"

By taking the false objection, "I need to think about it," and making it into something specific that you can handle (We are obviously presuming you know that your IT guys can install network cards on the printers or solve the issue in some other way), you can come up with a specific solution that ties the customer down. Insecure customers on the other hand, just want an excuse to delay a decision and tend to leap at any made-up objection you can throw at them.

The same strategy is very useful as a tool for setting up the next call you will make to a potential customer. Let's say you are unable to sell to the client in this call. The customer is not presenting her own specific, real objection but she is one of those people who will insist that she is not making a decision the same day and that "she needs some time to think about it." By inventing an objection and getting the customer to buy into it, you have set up a perfect scenario for your next call. Instead of a general "Hi Pam, have you had some time to look at our offer?" question, which tends to lead nowhere, you can start your next call with "As I recall it was really the lack of a network printing feature you were concerned about, right? Well, good news, Pam! I have spoken to our IT department and…"

The third type of situation when seller-created objections may be useful is for those leads you simply cannot get beyond the information stage. Whenever you try some trial close questions, they are clearly hesitant, and your call(s) keep consisting of you mostly talking about the product forever and ever. Again you can use a seller-created objection to postulate a non-existing problem as the final problem before you are ready to close a deal, then solve it and go straight on to a proper closing. If the customer starts complaining, you can always back down by saying something like "Oh, I'm sorry Pam. I thought the uncertainty about the networking abilities was what was preventing you guys from making a decision. We'll do this at your pace, of course."

Using price as a seller-created objection can be very tempting because price-based objections are so easy to handle for you as a seller. And when they work, they work very well. Price, however, in my experience can be very sensitive here because some potential customers will take it as an insult if you say, "I understand this may be too expensive for you guys." You risk the customer immediately coming back with "No, price isn't really an issue for us. Quality is what's important and we don't know you guys and your products at all." Unless the customer has given some indication that price might be a concern, making price a seller-created objection is, in my view, not a good idea.

"But without insurance, how would your wife carry on if you should die?"

"Well... I don't care as long as she behaves herself while I'm alive."

CUSTOMER PERSONALITIES

We've all had the experience of making a phone call or having a meeting that we're really not looking forward to, whether it is callback number 28 to a difficult lead, a follow-up call to a customer you are worried you oversold or a cold call to some important company. But then seconds after you start talking to the other person, you realize that "Hey, this guy is really easy to talk to!" And there is the opposite experience of calling a person whom you think will be really nice to talk to, and then realizing that "Damn, this isn't going well at all."

This happens all the time, but what is interesting—and what can really help your career—is realizing why it happens. The fact is that some people just talk well together and others don't. But since no one can make a career out of talking just to people with matching personalities, we need to understand how to adapt to different people and different situations. Some people are better at this than others by nature, but it is a skill that you can learn through a theoretical approach and a bit of practice.

People can work well together on many levels: same humor, same dialect and so on. But in my experience it is particularly the energy level and pace of people that determines whether they talk well together on the phone or not. If there is a huge mismatch in the natural pace and energy level between you and the potential customer, you need to adjust.

Sales and sales psychology books tend to divide people into groups based on their personality and behavior in a meeting situation. The number of groups varies wildly from just two to over twenty in some literature. I have always found that it is sufficient to talk about four main types of behavioral patterns. Nearly anyone you talk to, on the phone or in a meeting, will fit into one of these categories.

Let's start with the group that I personally have always found the easiest to talk to: the **Energetic Guy**.

> *All these categories of personalities obviously include women. However I find that in texts and lectures "the Energetic Guy" flows better and is easier to remember than "the Energetic Guy or Gal" or "energetic persons".*

The Energetic Guy has a high energy level and usually an optimistic view of life. You all know what sort of people I'm talking about—they will talk a lot, often at a very fast pace. Their positive attitude makes them very easy to talk to (they tend to want to do most of the talking), but also a constant source of disappointment. It is a constant source of amusement for seasoned sellers when a young, optimistic seller excitedly hangs up with an Energetic Guy and explains that, although he didn't actually buy today, because he was on his way into a meeting/didn't have his credit card on him/ didn't have access to a fax until tomorrow, "He is definitely buying tomorrow!" After a meeting or phone call with a lead of the Energetic Guy type, sellers tend to come out feeling really good about the call, thinking the deal is as good as in the box. Somehow, however, it rarely is with the Energetic Guy—at least not unless you know how to handle him.

The Energetic Guy usually has a problem with time management; he has a problem with promising too much and he has a problem with just forgetting the whole thing. So when you are dealing with an Energetic Guy, you really want to make sure you are organized for him. And you want to tie him down there and then—you want to make sure his promises are clear and, if at all possible, confirmed by email or fax as soon as possible.

The Energetic Guy is not the sort of person who takes notes from phone calls or meetings. And if he does he will probably lose them. So when you call back an Energetic Guy you need to make sure you are well prepared and you may want to start with a recap of what you have previously discussed and agreed. After a phone call it is probably a good idea to email him to confirm what you talked about, what you agreed and what the road forward is.

On the positive side, as long as you remain friendly and positive, you can be quite upfront with an Energetic Guy. These customers tend to ask questions or explore possibilities with your product during the call. Often they are as good as selling to themselves as you are—at least until you get to the actual commitment, the closing phase.

It is important to let this type of customer talk. They like to hear the sounds of their own voices and if you start talking too much, they tend to get bored and lose focus. Your job is simply to steer the conversation in the right direction.

While other customers might find you pushy if you call too frequent, the Energetic Guy tends not to have too much of a problem with this. This type of customer is in general more than happy to set aside 10 minutes every second day for the next two weeks. It's tying them down that is tricky. When talking on the phone with an Energetic Guy, remember to match the upbeat attitude and fast pace of the customer. Make sure to sound excited and use plenty of compliments in your conversation combined with positive "noises" of the "Ah!" and "Wow!" type. They like to feel valued so if you have a chance, ask them about their opinion or input.

Energetic Guys like to present themselves as likable and helpful, so they tend to respond well to direct questions for favors, such as "Could you do me a favor and look at the email I just sent you?" or "I really need to get this order in before the end of the month, so I'd appreciate it if you could fax it right back to me." For the same reason they are usually more than happy to provide you with referral business.

The second personality type I want to discuss is the **Business Guy**. The Business Guy, as the name indicates, is all about business. He makes quick and clear decisions; he is usually very opinionated—and when he's made up his mind, nothing you can do will make him change it again.

The Business Guy is very clear on what he likes and what he thinks is possible. But he or she (usually the former) may be very, very difficult to talk to. He is the sort of person who will shake his head while you talk, interrupt and in general feel much more difficult to handle than the Energetic Guy. You need to adapt your way of talking to the way Business Guys like to communicate. They do not want to hear about your fishing trip last week; they do not want a 20-minute PowerPoint of the background of your new product. They want to know what you can do for them. Get that right and you can easily sell on the first call.

Remember that the Business Guy often behaves in a way intended to test you. He may interrupt you or be extremely dismissive, just to see if you have courage and backbone. Don't get nervous and give up. Yet don't get too cocky with him either. Stick to a serious business tone in your communication and make sure you are well prepared even for a short follow-up call.

When you talk to a Business Guy, make sure you keep listening for signs that he has stopped paying attention and is now doing something else, like answering email. If you suspect that he isn't focusing on you, ask some intelligent, business-related "tell me" questions to engage him and make him focus on you.

If you push the right buttons and manage to show the Business Guy how he can benefit from your product, he is just a short step away from committing to buy. Unlike the Energetic Guy, if a Business Guy thinks something is to his benefit, he will want to go for it quickly.

The third personality type I want to discuss is the **Checklist Guy**. (Some sales books refer to them as "the Precise Customers.") The Checklist Guy is a stickler for details and needs every little box on the form ticked before he or she (quite often the latter) moves on. You tend to find such personalities in middle management positions, but even highly successful businessmen can have this type of personality. They never make a decision based on gut feelings or because they "just like you." When you communicate with a Checklist Guy, make sure you don't get overly enthusiastic; talk slowly and in a structured way and above all be well-prepared. (The Checklist Guy tends to do a lot of research.)

The good thing about Checklist Guys is that they can shop with their heads rather than their hearts. When you realize this, it all boils down to a proper needs analysis and then showing that you or your project ticks all the right boxes. Handle the Checklist Guy this way, and you will find him or her a very easy partner to work with.

When you work with a Checklist Guy, focus on making him talk about his needs early on in the call. This will give you material to build up a logical argument for him to buy. Use those needs as bullet points later to show why it will benefit him to go for your product or service.

Easily confused with the Checklist Guy type of customer is the **Hesitant Guy.** These have many of the same traits as the standard Checklist Guy, but are so insecure that even good logical arguments may not be sufficient. Because they are so insecure and scared of committing to a deal, they tend to want to talk to a third party—usually someone who is in no better position to help them make a decision than themselves. They will call their mothers to ask advice on life insurance, their auditor to discuss office printers and their lawyers to discuss pest control. This is obviously not good for you as a salesperson as it leaves you without any control or influence over the final decision-making progress. None of the resources—his mother, auditor or lawyer —has any particular reason to suggest he agrees to your solution, and in my experience third parties in general tend to be hesitant suggesting that a friend or colleague sign a deal they know little about. First of all they have not been part of the initial discussion, so are not influenced by your sales pitch at all, and secondly saying "No, don't do it" seems to be a safer choice than saying "Yes, go for it!" It is simply less risky for them. If they suggest doing nothing, then it is unlikely that a clearly identifiable problem is going to occur in the near future for which they can be held responsible. If they suggest signing a contract, on the other hand, you may turn out to be a scam artist or swindler (They don't know you and most likely have no idea who your company is) which will make them look like idiots. So letting a lead go away and discuss it with random third parties is likely to have disastrous effects on your chances of closing a deal. The way to prevent this is to very quickly in the call identify these extremely insecure customers and spend a lot of time reassuring the lead with phrases like "We will help you all the way, "Most of our customers go for the Zuper Printer X1," "We'll talk tomorrow and go through the entire process together" and so on. By constantly reassuring the lead that this is safe and this is what nearly everyone does these days, you will gradually reduce their nervousness and make them feel that you are the guy who will take care of them. This way hopefully the lead will not feel the need to talk things over with random people before making a final decision.

"Buy the fucking vacuum cleaner or the dog gets it!"

LINGUISTIC AND LOGICAL TRICKS

As I mentioned early in this book, good selling today is not about tricking anyone into accidentally saying "yes." The introduction of consumer protection laws, more alert customers and the exposure to reputation damage online mean that good selling today is more than ever about actually convincing the customer. If you only use clever tricks to get your orders you'll probably have an angry client calling you 15 minutes from now. You need to convince him that your product is the right thing for him (and ideally also convince him that he selected the product himself).

This means that pure linguistic magic tricks are perhaps less part of a good sales strategy than several decades ago. Still, however, using simple linguistic techniques can help you save time when presenting your arguments, handle some objections more efficiently and control the call better.

You already know one linguistic trick: the use of questions at the end of every sentence, to keep control and better predict what the customer will say next. Another equally basic trick to keep control, although perhaps more practical than linguistic, is to ask the potential customer to do something you know the outcome of. Let's say you are worried you are losing control of a conversation because you can feel the customer becoming bored or starting to focus on something else. By asking him to perform a simple task that you control or know the outcome of, you can get his focus back and steer the conversation away from riskier subjects:

SELLER: "So, as I said, John, these printers will improve your productivity, as I am sure, right?"

CUSTOMER: "Mmm."

SELLER: "And the duplex printing for drafts will also considerably reduce your cost, agreed?"

CUSTOMER: "Mmm, um, yeah…"

SELLER: "Tell me, John, you said you're sitting by your computer right now. Just so I know what sort of print drivers you use today, could you open your 'Device and Printers' and then read out the name of the printer devices listed there? What printer names do you see there?"

CUSTOMER: "What, um, sure. Hang on."

The seller realized he was losing the lead here. The lead wasn't listening and the seller had to do something to avoid the dreaded "Could you send me some information on email?" which would surely have come any minute now. The seller may not have known exactly what printers the lead would find in his Device and Printers tab but it was safe to presume that the information was not going to negatively influence the chance of closing a deal.

Building trust is obviously important in sales, and on the phone there are a few linguistic tricks you can use to subconsciously make the potential customer trust you better. One of the most basic tricks you can use to encourage trust is based on the principles of social categorization. This is basically a subconscious division of people into groups, with increased loyalty and trust felt for someone within the same group. By using personal pronouns inclusively, such as referring to "we," "us" and "ours" in a sense that includes both you and the customer, the customer subconsciously sees you and him as part of the same team and automatically tends to trust you more.

Another trick to build trust is based on what is known as the "Uncertainty Reduction" in communication theory. The theory itself is a rather complex set of presumptions of behavior in social interaction developed in the late '70s by two scientists, Charles Berger and Richard Calabrese, at Northwestern University. For the purposes of this book, however, it is sufficient to know that the theory is based on the fact that in the initial stages of interaction between two strangers, there is a considerable degree of stress and uncertainty due to the lack of previous knowledge of the other person, making predictions of his or her behavior impossible. By volunteering information about yourself, uncertainty is reduced and replaced by a feeling of increased trust. A number of studies have found that the mere act of telling more, whether true or untrue, can reduce uncertainty and increase trust. This doesn't mean that as a seller you should start talking in length about yourself, your hobbies and your family and health. But it does mean that it is important to get a good conversation going. And gradually, as part of a natural flow of the conversation you should try to provide information about your company and how you work.

> *Interestingly, and here we move from the proper Uncertainty Reduction Theory and into my own years of experience with sales and contract negotiations, the uncertainty reduction works even if the disclosure is done by the customer. The mere act of talking about oneself seems to help reduce anxiety and increase trust. Just allowing and encouraging the customer to talk about himself and his company, in my experience, helps the customer to feel he can trust you.*

A third technique to build trust between you and the customer is to avoid using general terms and instead use language as specific as possible. Instead of saying things like

"These printers will certainly help your company" you should be as clear as possible about the benefits. Use more specific phrases such as "These printers will reduce your printing costs because they use much less ink than standard printers" or "These printers will improve your efficiency because of their intelligent printer queue handling." It is much easier to believe something specific than something general when coming from a stranger, and constant use of such specific language tend to build trust.

Another linguistic trick to control a call is the use of manipulative question phraseology. This basically falls into two separate categories of techniques: using questions with a false or premature premise and using questions with answer alternatives that are unnaturally limiting.

Asking "When we install the printers, would you like us to include some additional print trays?" to a customer who hasn't yet ordered is obviously using a premise that may not be true. The whole question takes it for granted that the customer will buy. From a sales technical point of view, however, such questions can be very efficient. Structuring your question in this way achieves several things. By repeatedly referring to the (false) premise that the customer is buying, subconsciously the customer will become used to the idea and accept the premise as true. In addition the question is controlling, and by answering such questions, the customer subconsciously ties himself down. It is obviously meaningless to say that he wants additional print trays delivered with the printers if he isn't buying in the first place. Gradually for each such question it becomes more and more difficult for the customer to say "I need to think about it" or "Send me a brochure." He is de facto committed to placing an order. And finally you keep control of the call because you know exactly what the customer is going to say, even before you ask the question (in this example either "Yes" or "No").

The second question technique, with answer alternatives that are unnaturally limiting, can be equally efficient. The principle is simple. When asking a question make sure you set two alternatives that are either both to your advantage or one alternative that is clearly unacceptable and another that is to your advantage:

"When we deliver the printers, would you prefer our free installation service or will you be doing the installation yourself?"

In either case you are presuming that he will buy the printers, and by selecting either of the alternative answers given, the customer ties himself down.

"Would you, at this stage, say that it is more important for you to stick with a technology you know from before, or would you be interested in increased efficiency and a significant lowering of cost?"

Here the potential customer is given one choice which is obviously ridiculous, to stick to what he has at all costs, and a clearly preferable choice of doing more at a lower cost. Should the customer insist that he wants to stick to what he has, he is clearly being difficult just to be difficult, and you need to work on building trust. It is a safe bet that the huge majority of customers are going to say they prefer increased efficiency and a lowering of cost.

Interestingly such question techniques are also part of the so called Reid technique which is used as an interrogation technique by law enforcement officers in many US states. While controlling the outcome of a sales call is obviously to the benefit of the seller, one might ask if the same is really true for an interviewing police officer. In any case their training videos are a useful study for a phone seller; they can sometimes be found available online.

Be careful not to dumb down your questions too much. If asked "Do you prefer to buy bad printers at a high cost or good printers cheaply from us" not only do you treat the customer as a fool, you are also coming off quite confrontational.

Among other logical or linguistic tricks are so-called fallacies: building logical arguments based on false premises or false logical steps. A fallacy uses a proper logical argument, but the conclusion is drawn based on facts that are not real. The logic is there, but the end result is based on false premises or false facts. "As you say, your current supplier is 10% more expensive than us, so it is pretty obvious that we are the cheapest option for your new printers." It does sound appealingly logical, but this statement is obviously based on the presumption that the customer has to choose between only his current supplier and you. Obviously that is usually not the case—there are probably hundreds of companies out there that can supply the customer with his printers. The use of such a fallacy does not necessarily mean that the conclusion is wrong—you may in fact be the cheapest supplier out there—but it does base itself on a logical shortcut to convince the customer of this.

Similar in result to basing correct logical reasoning on false facts, is using faulty logical reasoning based on true facts: "Our printers are more than twice as fast as your current printers, so as you can understand they are going to lower your printing costs significantly." Again it may sound convincing, and it may very well be true, but in reality there is of course no guaranteed logical correlation between printing speed and printing cost.

Another logical fallacy is the use of comparisons with false equivalence: You deliberately compare oranges with apples. The result can be either correct or incorrect—the point is that the logic is incorrect. You may want to use this logical fallacy to present true facts, but in a way that is easier to explain. The more complicated the products, the easier to play around with such figures. But even with something simple as printing, you could pull out your own printer's black-and-white printing speed, and compare it with competitors' color printing speed.

Perhaps the most commonly encountered fallacy, both in sales and in everyday life, is the use of what is known as "bandwagoning." By creating the impression that something is very common, you give the customer a feeling of false security (It must be safe since many people do this), and perhaps even a degree of pressure to jump on something for fear of missing out. As an example: "OK, so we are delivering those printers on Friday. Just one more thing: Practically all our Zuper Laser X1 customers opt for the tray upgrade package. It allows the printer to sort and stack prints (…)" By saying that practically everyone who has opted for the same printer as his choice also buy the tray upgrade package, you create a degree of stress for the customer. If he doesn't buy this, will the printers really be that useful for him? If everyone is doing it, it must be good.

The final fallacy I want to mention is "term manipulation." By using manipulative terms or names to describe products and services you can make them seem more attractive than they really are. The shampoo and makeup businesses are really the best examples I can think of here: Eye Studio Master, Instant Age Rewind, Professional Studio and so on. Just because someone sticks "professional studio" in the product name, it may still be cheap or poor-quality goods. But the trick works. The mind somehow automatically presumes it is a better product just because the brand name contains the word "professional." In a sales call you can use this trick on a smaller scale, for example by referring to competitors' prices as "costs" while referring to your own prices as "investments": "As you will have seen from the presentation I sent you, the

Evil Competitor X1 will cost more than $900 per unit. With the discount I have offered you, you can get 10 of our Pro1 units for a total investment of $5,500."

As I have pointed out repeatedly in this book, the way the world works today, it is usually not a good idea for either you or your company to use blatant tricks to make customers sign up for products they don't need nor want. Yet, as a seller, linguistic and logic tricks may come in handy to simplify parts of your pitch. If your company and your competitors both use complicated pricing structures that would take ages to explain (and lengthy technical monologues rarely leads to sales), you may want to simplify both your and their pricing structures to replicate the facts in a more understandable way. More important, though, is that a good understanding of such logical and linguistic tricks may help you recognize them if used against you by a potential customer. Some customers just want to challenge what you are saying, but often they have spoken to other sellers or read other companies' marketing material. If you can recognize logical and linguistic fallacies, it may help you handle objections that would otherwise be difficult to manage.

> *Let's say a lead says something like "Well, I really like your printer product, but you guys are basing the setup on a Unix print server, and today most companies are opting for Windows-based options." Your brain should now go ding-ding-ding: This is pure bandwagoning. Instead of arguing about the facts ("Well, I'm not sure about that, John"), you could use your understanding of the logical fault in the customer's argument as a basis for a good, convincing comeback: "I understand your concerns, John. Yet I think the real question here is 'What will benefit your company the most?' and there I am sure you agree with me that a Unix-based solution will be both more flexible and more efficient."*

> *Or let's presume a customer states "I like your Super Printer X1. But I think we really need a professional solution, so we are leaning toward Evil Competitor Professional." You explain*

nicely and in a non-confrontational way that Evil Competitor Professional may have the word "professional" in it, but if we examine the actual specifications in detail we will see Super Printer 1X is clearly the more advanced product.

"Eh, great question! Come to think of it, I am not really sure what I'm trying to sell you".

ADVANCED SKILLS

HOW TO SELL ON FOLLOW-UP CALLS

If you fine-tune your sales skills with the advice in this book, you will find that you close more and more sales on your first calls. For a great seller, the first call offers a unique chance to get the potential customer excited and carried along, and caught sufficiently off-guard on the closing to actually confirm the order there and then.

No matter how good you are, though, some leads will require one or more follow-up calls. This is where a lot of phone sellers collapse completely. I have seen brilliant cold callers lose all their self-confidence and forget all sales strategy on their follow-up calls.

First of all: don't just pick up the phone and hope for a miracle. This seems to be the main strategy of a lot of sellers: Bud Wiezer didn't buy on the first call, but if I call him again now maybe he has magically changed his mind. This bingo-lottery approach to selling will lead to much disappointment and frustration.

I always recommend writing a sales script even for your second calls. This can be much less formal and less detailed than your first call script, but as for your standard pitch, writing things down tends to make you think them through in more detail. Your follow-up script can be just some loose ideas and drafts for how you may want to open and how you may want to get the customer from the informal chatty phase into a closing phase. But just having a script in front of you will help you focus on sales strategy and prevent you from having those calls where you just chat for 15 minutes, both agreeing it has been a pleasant talk, and then say goodbye without being any closer to a sale.

The important thing to remember about a follow-up call is that *this potential customer did not buy last time.* This leads to the natural question "Why should he buy now?" If you can't answer that, you shouldn't call him. Before you call him you need to find out what is going to trigger him to buy now.

The best way to prepare for a follow-up call is to end the first call properly. This way one call lines up for a close in the next call. You do this by actively identifying what is preventing the customer from buying in one call, and calling back when that issue has been solved (or calling back to suggest a solution to the issue). If the customer had a clear reason not to commit last time, like having to talk to his IT guys about their current printer setup, or getting approval to spend the money from his boss, then fine. It is clear what has to be handled before you can close a deal. Sadly most people don't really know what caused them not to buy, any more than most people really know what caused them to buy. People, like deities, generally work in mysterious ways. As a seller it is your job to identify the reason for not closing in one call, so that you can use that to close the next time you call back. You don't want to leave a customer just "thinking about it." This is perhaps the most commonly made mistake ruining follow-up calls. A potential customer says he "needs to think about it" and the seller, perhaps after a few more attempts on closing, simply says "Sure, I understand that." But where does that leave you for a follow-up call? You can ask if the customer has had time to think about it, but that is totally out of your control. Most customers will have spent a total of exactly nil minutes and zilch seconds thinking about you and your offer after you hung up. Let's be honest; people do not hang up with a phone seller, close the door to their office and tell their secretaries, "Anna Logue, hold all calls for the next two days. I need to think about an offer from this Dan Druff guy from Dan Druff Printers." Most of the time, when you hang up, people simply go "Damn, I need to get myself an unlisted number."

So you really want to prod the lead for more information about what he wants to "think about." This can be difficult because people in general don't know themselves and you don't want to be rude or too pushy. Nor do you want to ask leading questions because people will jump on any excuse to get you off the line.

The best way to analyze the problem is to listen to the customer: what he says, when he says it and how he says it. Often you will feel that the customer is engaged and keen, but then suddenly his answers get reduced to "Mmm" and "Um, yes" and similar grunt-like responses. Was it something in the call at this point that made him cautious? An intelligent, experienced seller will often have some instinct about where the customer is lost. Use this actively to obtain more information about the problem. Ask open questions at this point like "How does that sound to you, Barry?" or "Based on what I've told you so far, Barry, how do you feel about our printers and what they can do for your company?" With a bit of luck, Barry will say something like "It sounds good, but I am a little bit concerned about the price" or "To be honest, I fear that your price is much higher than what we pay at the moment." That is great because it gives you something to work within that call and something to work with on your follow-up.

If you just get a general "I need to think about it," you should ask politely for more details. No one just needs to "think about it." What on earth is "it" anyway? Don't say that, of course, but ask questions like "I fully understand that, Barry.

What are the main things we need to clarify for you?" or "Of course, Barry! Talk me through the things you feel you need more information about." Try to avoid asking deeply negative questions like "What are you worried about?" "What is the main problem preventing you from buying?" and the sales killer of all sales killers "Why won't you commit today?" which is basically a short version of "OK, give me ten reasons why you should not buy from me today."

If your gentle prodding leads to no more information about what the customer wants to think about, there is an emergency strategy you can use to at least line up a decent opening for your next call. As I mentioned above, if you ask a leading question at this stage, most customers will jump at it because they see an easy way to end the call. You can use that to tie the customer down to a specific problem that you can solve. You can say things like "OK, I understand, Barry. I guess one of your main concerns is that our printers may not fit into your current technical solution" or "Sure, Barry. I guess one of the things you really want to make sure of is that our printers meet your requirements when it comes to speed and toner usage," etc. The potential customer will usually be so grateful for any excuse that he is likely to say "Yes, exactly. I really need to check that before I can commit to anything." This way you have a clearly identifiable strategy for your next call. When you make that follow-up call, you can have prepared yourself with print speed and toner usage statistics or say that you have spoken to your IT guys and they can confirm that your printers will work well in his current IT setup. But the main point is that you get an opener; you can immediately start the call like this:

"Hi Barry Cade! This is Dick Tator from Don Key, Inc."
"Um, OK?"
"We spoke last Monday regarding improving your printer and photocopier infrastructure."
"Oh, yes, I…"

"Now, you asked me to look into the integration issue to make sure your new equipment would work well with your current IT setup. The issue was really if your Ubuntu machines would work with our standard printer servers, and our IT guys have now confirmed this is not an issue—they will integrate seamlessly! Just one quick question: you mentioned you also have some desktop printers not connected to your network at all. Can you tell me a little bit more about this?"

You can thus use the information from the previous call to make sure you get your foot well in the door. And because you have solved the lead's problem, it is also going to be much more difficult for him again to attempt to delay the decision.

In some cases you may have sent out a brochure, an email or some other sort of informative material. This can work well: When a potential customer sees a physical brochure it moves your company from the mystical and intangible phone and Internet world into the world of bricks and stone. It is much easier for a customer to trust your company when he has seen some physical material, no matter what it is. Suddenly he has some proof of your existence, and this tends to remove much of the hesitation many potential customers may have with entering into contracts with you or giving you credit card details. Somehow it feels safer when he has seen some physical evidence of your existence.

This is, of course, much more a mental thing than a real assurance. Even if someone has printed proper brochures he may still be a scam artist. But all statistical evidence seems to indicate that receiving a physical brochure significantly improves the trust between you and your customer.

Such brochures and information emails carry with them one inherent danger, though. Few leads will actually read your brochure thoroughly, but it does give them a perfect excuse to delay the decision-making process by saying "Sorry, but I haven't had time to look at what you sent me yet. Can you call next week?" To avoid this you want to take it absolutely for granted that the customer has both received and read your brochure or email. Don't ask "Did you get my email?" Simply presume that he has read it and start your pitch. If a customer says "I haven't had time to read your email" try to counter it with something like "Sure, no problem, Barry. I'll talk you through the information. But can I just ask you a quick question regarding your current printer infrastructure? You said that you had some desktop printers not connected to the network at all. Can you tell me how these are being used by your staff today?"

Now, after we have managed to open the call properly and gotten the customer talking, comes the real challenge of the follow-up call. We really want to be able to bring something new into the call. We do *not* want the second and third call to sound like lightly modified versions of the first call. This, however, can be a challenge. If you got the first call going well, you may easily have brought him well into your closing phase and used most of your standard questions and pitch. Before you call you must think through what you will discuss with the customer and how you intend to bring him along to your closing form. And when you get to those closing questions (see page 92), you want to make sure it sounds natural. If you asked him for a physical delivery address, don't ask him again in the same way. And don't just confirm the information by going "You said your office address is Bingo Street 1, right?" Try to add a new twist to the form by saying things like "OK. Last time you said your office is in Bingo Street 1. Would that be just by the Golf Shop on 22nd Street?" or "You confirmed to me last time that you preferred the off-white version. Would you be looking to buy all the printers in the same color?" This way you avoid the second call being a silly repetition of your first. Of course if you got stuck early on in the information phase on the first call, this is much less of an issue.

This brings us to the last important success factor for follow-up calls: your notes. Whether you keep notes on pieces of paper, Post-its or in a proper digital CRM system, you must make sure you keep sufficient notes on your customer interaction to make the next call a good one. I am constantly surprised by how many potentially brilliant sellers ignore this. You must remember that while you make perhaps 10, 20 or 50 calls in a day, the potential customer spoke to you only once. You may not recall what you discussed and how you sounded, but the customer will. And if you rattle off a mere repeat of your first call, he will just think you're an idiot seller who cares nothing about him or his needs and just wants to dump a worthless product on him. Any trust will be lost and so will your commission.

Among those sellers who do keep notes, I am further surprised by how bad those notes sometimes are. Notes on pieces of paper tend to be incomprehensible drivel decorated with doodles of flowers and parts of the seller's own pitch, and notes in proper CRM systems tends to be irrelevant nonsense like "Customer used to work for LAPD" and "He is closed next Monday." What you want to write down are those things that can make your next call great. This includes:

How far you got on your pitch.
What issues arose during the call that may prevent the customer from buying (objections and obstacles).
Good reasons for the customer to buy that came up during the call.
Customer's current situation in relation to what you sell.
Anything that you agreed you would look into before your next call.
Anything that you have sent or emailed to the customer.
The customer personality type (e.g. Energetic Guy)
Anything the customer agreed to do before your follow-up call (like checking something with his IT department).

These are notes that you can look at before your follow-up call and use to tailor your follow-up pitch to this customer, therefore maximizing your chances of closing.

CONFERENCE CALLS: HOW TO SELL TO GROUPS

Selling to a group of people, whether in a traditional phone conference or on a video or Skype conference, involves some specific challenges that a regular one-to-one phone call does not.

There are many different strategies for conference calls, but essentially you want to keep the same sales focus in such calls as you have in a one-to-one call. Sadly there is a tendency for sellers to forget all sales technique when moving into conference selling. Instead, conference calls tend to turn into some sort of lecture, with longwinded PowerPoint presentations. This is a bad idea—the focus still needs to be on selling.

When you are dealing with a group of people, it is important that you quickly attempt to identify each person's position in the team. Who are they, what do they do and what is their status and role in the decision-making process?

One of the first things you need to identify is whether there is a clearly identifiable decision-maker in the group. This can sometimes be very easy. If you're having a conference call with an IT guy, a guy from Finance and the CEO of the company, you will normally presume the CEO to be the decision-maker.

Even when there is a clearly identifiable person in charge, you need to listen closely to their internal communication during the conference call, though. Some bosses rely heavily on the advice of key staff, so in the end it may be that the easiest way of securing a sale is to convince that person. Listen for the top person asking questions or constantly involving someone else in the discussion. It may be that she feels uncomfortable making a decision herself, not necessarily because she is a weak manager, but because the topic of discussion may be way outside her expertise. The more complex the product or service you're offering, the more likely a manager is to rely on expert staff like the head of IT, the in-house lawyer and so on.

You should also listen actively to see if you can identify any potential troublemakers. In a conference call with many departments represented, you may find that one of the departments finds what you are offering a threat to their position in the company. If you are selling IT support services, for example, you may find that the head of IT is delighted because it will take some pressure off his department, or you may find that he feels that your services will weaken his department's position in the company. Listen for people who ask questions with a negative spin. Most questions can be asked in a neutral way, such as "Will your printer server increase our maintenance costs?" or in a negative way, such as "Your printer server will increase our maintenance costs, won't it?" A person who repeatedly asks questions with a negative spin may be biased against you or the products or service you offer. If you do identify a potential troublemaker, listen to how others communicate with him and how others try to include or exclude him from the discussion. He may have a weak position in the company or he may have a strong position.

Keeping control of a conference call can be much more difficult than keeping control of a one-to-one phone call. There are many people who may want to add something to the discussion so predicting where a call is heading may be difficult.

In general you should encourage a more loose dialogue than in one-to-one calls. Encouraging input and brainstorming may not exactly keep you in control as such, but it may lead to the others discussing among themselves, leaving you on the outside to just gently steer the discussion in the right direction. What you want to avoid is every team member bombarding you with questions. If you are reduced to just answering questions, you won't be able to drive the call forward.

> *Video conferences are great because you can now see the participants' body language and use that to read what they think and how they may feel about you, your product and your pitch at any given time. It falls outside the scope of this book to go into detail on this, but there are plenty of good books on sales and body language out there. There is one important thing to remember as a phone seller, though, if you suddenly find yourself in a video conference: Not only can you see them; they can see you too. Phone sellers have a tendency to develop very odd behaviors because they sit visually isolated from their customers day after day. Some phone sellers crouch down clasping their headsets when they start the closing phase, some walk around obsessively waving their hands and some just put their feet on the table and try to clean their nails with a broken pen. This can look extremely odd when you're suddenly on a video link. Whatever your habits are, make sure you focus on your body language and your visual behavior when you do video conferences.*

Groups tend to be much more indecisive than individuals and there tends to be more confusion. Typically when one person stops talking there will be long pauses, without anyone wanting to take charge, or people will all of a sudden start talking at the same time. As a seller you can use this inherent indecisiveness to take charge. If there is some confusion on the other team on who should be talking next, take control by saying things like "I guess one of the things you guys really want to know about is the print server implementation" or "I guess our intelligent printer queue system is one of the things that may be important for you guys, so let me just briefly explain."

In a one-to-one call you can use questions to keep good control of the customer. By asking questions all the time, you can make sure you know what he will be saying next because instead of making up his own questions or comments he is focusing on answering you. This can be much more difficult in a conference call. As when a teacher asks a tricky question to his class and every pupil suddenly either looks very busy trying to find something in his bag or tries to become as invisible as possible by sinking in to his chair, a group in a conference call may decide to just stare at the table when you ask a question. This can be due to no one wanting to risk answering incorrectly and looking like a fool or it can be that no one feels the question is really within his field of expertise or job scope. In any case the fact is that when a question is asked to a group there is much less pressure on answering than if a question is asked one-to-one. Such situations can be awkward and embarrassing, and if people feel uncomfortable the probably won't buy from you. What you want to do is to early on try to identify people's roles in the company and then ask your question to one specific person. Make sure you have made some notes of each person's name at the start of the call, or you will find this difficult or impossible to do ("Hey you, yeah, you there on the left" is not a phrase that can be calculated to increase confidence and trust). Ask questions like "John, from an IT perspective, how does your department feel about moving all desktop printers to a single printer network" or "Peter, from a finance perspective, what features would you think would be the most essential to reduce your workload?"

One thing to remember for video conferences is that the camera location and the screen location can be very different. So don't try to look or point at the person you are addressing. On their end you may come out looking in completely the wrong direction. It's better to just look fairly straight into the camera and identify people clearly by name if you're addressing one specific person. It is also a fact, and one that most people tend to forget, that since screens in general are 2-D, if you point to the left of center, you are in fact pointing left of everyone regardless of where they are in the room (even the ones sitting to the left). This can cause some confusion and make you look very odd indeed.

Try to engage the whole group during a video conference. Not only does this tend to make everyone feel valued (and thus more positive toward you and your product) but it also makes it easier for you to identify problems. The head of IT, for example, may not be the sort of person who likes to speak in a group, but after the call has ended he may tell his boss that he is concerned about this and that and thus either cost you the sale or lead to a delayed decision.

Use more complex questions than you would in a normal phone call. "You see what I mean?" and "This makes sense, right?" may work well to control a customer on a phone call, but they will just seem like rhetorical questions in a conference call. Use a lot of "Tell me…" and "Could you explain to me?" questions. There are usually one or two people in a conference call anxious to show off in front of their manager, so if you push the right buttons they may answer in detail and give you time to plan your next move.

Control the group and make sure everyone remains interested by moving from one person to the other. Say things like "Let me just try to establish how you guys work today. John, you're the IT expert; can you briefly explain your current printer infrastructure?" Then move on to Pam the head of finance and Roger the head of sales and so on. Not only does this keep everyone focused and ensure everyone feels valued, but it also establishes you as the maestro, the conductor in charge of the conference call. This is essential for your chances of success.

When you have done a round of questions, try to draw some intelligent overall conclusion: "OK, from what you guys are telling me it seems pretty clear that what we need to focus on is, one, to reduce the printer queues so that people don't have to wait by the printer for several minutes like today; and, two, to make sure that the overall printing costs are reduced. Right?" This makes you not only seem like you have taken everyone's input seriously, but it also raises you to a level above the various departmental disagreements and squabbles. This can appeal very much to whoever is the final decision-maker.

If you are going to go for a closing during your conference call, start moving toward that close by asking some follow-up questions to those participants who have seemed the most positive. Use trial close questions like "John, as the IT expert, from what you have heard today, would you say that the Super Laser X1 meets your basic requirements well?" Getting positive answers from these easy-to-convince participants ties down the final decision-maker. If several members of the group have given positive answers to your trial close questions, it appears as if the group is ready to sign a deal. If he does not proceed, it will seem like he is going against the advice of the group.

If there is a clearly identifiable decision-maker, like a CEO or high level manager, flatter him by asking your final closing questions to him. Make it clear to everyone that the decision is his and his alone: "John, this is obviously up to you. I think we have established that we can offer you guys some clear advantages over what you have today. Do you think we are ready to proceed?" If you have built up to this question well, the risk should be minimal. At the same time it is essential to make it clear that you haven't tried to trick anyone into an order they don't want. In one-to-one calls we often try to avoid asking the direct question, and just take down the order (see page 92). But because this is almost impossible to do with a whole group of people in a conference call, I find that this strategy works best.

GATEKEEPERS

When trying to build a career as a seller, you will very soon realize that between you and your commission stand not only the real decision-maker, but a large group of receptionists, switchboard operators, PAs and secretaries. As a group, these people can appear hell-bent on preventing you from getting through to the people who actually matter. We usually refer to these people as "gatekeepers," although much worse descriptions can be heard in sales offices around the world on bad days.

First of all it is important to understand why the gatekeepers are there in the first place. You can be pretty sure they are not there solely to annoy you—although it may feel like they are—so you need to understand the gatekeeper's role in the company. This is important partly in order to bypass the gatekeeper, partly to work with the gatekeeper when you are unable to bypass him or her and partly to make sure you don't bypass a gatekeeper who might turn out to be the de facto decision-maker.

So let's look at the different types of gatekeepers. First you have the **Human Switchboard**. (It sounds degrading, I know, but it is the easiest way of describing them so that you understand what they do). These are basically people whose job it is to say "Welcome to Dr. Franklin Stein's office (...) hold on one moment and I'll put you through." In companies where the decision-maker is receiving a lot of calls, be it from sellers or customers, they will, however, quite often have been given some basic screening duties. These people have only a few seconds to decide whether they think you are worth the decision-maker's time, so getting your opening phrase right is vital.

These Human Switchboards will usually be looking for clues in how you present yourself and how you ask for the decision-maker. A trick that often works with larger companies is to make it sound like you've just talked to the decision-maker you are trying to reach. "Hi, it's John again," is often a good start. For a smaller company with a single operator, this may not be a good idea though, for obvious reasons. Some preparation is vital too: never, ever ask for a person by his role; ask for a person by his name. So don't say, "Could you put me through to your director of marketing, please?" Say, "Is Dan Saul Knight around?" If you seem to know Dan, it is natural for the operator to presume Dan knows you too.

Many gatekeepers of this type have been instructed to ask you for your reason for calling. Be prepared for this. You do not want to sound insecure or like you are hiding something. I find that a partial disclosure here works best, unless of course you do in fact have a very, very good reason for calling. "It's regarding your printer servers," is better than "I'm calling from Cheap Printers Inc., and I'd like to talk to him about buying some new printers from us." Sometimes, you may have sent the decision-maker an email beforehand, and then it is usually acceptable to describe it as an ongoing discussion. "It's regarding the new printer setup I have been discussing with him," might work quite well in such situations.

A different and perhaps more challenging type of gatekeeper is the **Assistant**. These can be PAs or administrative or executive assistants. Although their exact role in an organization varies, these people have a much closer relationship with the decision-maker and won't so easily fall for simple tricks. They usually know whom their boss has spoken to and what project the boss is involved in. The best strategy is to treat these people as decision-makers in their own right. You basically have to pitch your idea to them first and get them on board. This will not only make them feel important and respected, but it will also hopefully help gain you important allies. If you do your job right and sell the product, service or concept to the Assistant, he will often do the actual sales job for you. In many cases, he is in fact the de facto decision-maker unless you are talking about some very important project.

As I said, however, the actual importance of the Assistant varies from company to company. It is important to try to find out exactly what influence the person has. If you have sold the idea to the Assistant, but then still get no positive confirmation back that the boss is on board, you need to convince the Assistant to let you talk directly with the decision-maker.

Another type of gatekeeper is the **Researcher**. Such people usually have a dedicated screening job, and this makes it even more important to treat them as decision-makers in their own right. Again you should make a full disclosure of why you are calling or visiting and you should pitch the idea directly to them as you would pitch it to their boss. Never underestimate the importance and influence of the Researchers! In the vast majority of cases, their recommendation is followed by the decision-maker.

The final type of gatekeepers I want to mention is the **Partner.** In many smaller companies a decision-maker may just forward his phone to a colleague or business partner when he is out, or a colleague may just answer the phone on the decision-maker's desk when he or she hears the phone ringing. Their actual relationship with and influence over the decision-maker will vary hugely. It is therefore often best to just try to establish how or when you can reach the actual decision-maker. The best approach is a friendly tone combined with minimum disclosure: "Hi! This is John calling. I was trying to reach Peter?" Again this gives the impression that you are a friend of the decision-maker and since this person is answering someone else's phone he or she will most likely not want to insult you. When you have introduced yourself like this, simply ask when Peter will be in. Asking for a mobile number might sometimes work, but the downside is that a lot of people are very restrictive about giving out colleagues' phone numbers—and if you really were a close friend, you'd probably have it already.

NEW TECHNOLOGIES

Voicemail has become a standard part of every business telephone system. For an ambitious seller, however, it can be both a blessing and a curse.

Most professional sellers generally try to avoid leaving a voicemail message. The reason is simple: when leaving a voicemail you announce that you have called and basically hand away the control of the future communication, or at least the next step, to the other person. If you leave a message asking for a callback, you need to give the person time to actually call you back. It would be seen as rude leaving such a message, and then again making another call yourself 30 minutes later. This can seriously delay progress in closing a deal; even if you wait for a reasonable amount of time before calling again, you can easily be dismissed with a simple, "Yeah, John, I got your message. I'll call you back as soon as I have had more time to look at this." So the general rule, if you want to keep in control of the progress of the deal, is to simply not leave a message.

Sometimes, however, leaving a message is something that cannot be avoided. Either because you have unsuccessfully tried to reach the person many times, or because you for one reason or another need to announce that you have called (for example because you had agreed to call back at a specific time). In those cases you need to use the voicemail as a sales tool—to use that technology to your advantage.

When you leave a message on a voicemail, always make sure to adapt your message style to the personality of the person you are calling. If you have already spoken to the person, hopefully you have made a mental note of the type of person you are dealing with (see page 131). Was he an Energetic Guy, a Business Guy, a Checklist guy or a Hesitant Guy?

If you are calling for the first time, listen carefully to the voicemail greeting. The Energetic Guy is usually quite easy to recognize, even on a recording of just a few seconds. Typically they will sound upbeat, humorous, and often a bit roundabout in their message. A typical message will sound like "Hi there! You've just reached Peter! I'm obviously doing something very important now, but if you leave your name and phone number, I'll call you right back." If you adapt your message to Peter's upbeat style, you are much more likely to get a call back: "Hi Peter! It's Justin. I've got some great news regarding the network printers we talked about last week and really want to discuss this with you, so give me a call back at 555-8888. That's 555-8888."

The Business Guy, on the other hand, will have a very short message, straight to the point. Often they will even leave their default automated message. These guys either don't have the time, or at least pretend not to have the time, to record long, funny greetings. Leave a message in the same style: "Justin Time calling. I have some news on the printers we have discussed. Give me a call as soon as you can at 555-8888. That's 555-8888."

Finally the Hesitant Guy and the Checklist Guy: They will sound very neutral in their greeting. Such personalities will use standard phrases and usually include their full name: "You've reached Pat Hiscock. Leave a message after the tone." Don't leave long messages here. Just make sure to speak slowly and clearly when you leave a message for this type of person: "Hi, Pat. It's John. Just wanted to get back to you regarding some new information on the printer servers we discussed last week. Give me a call at 555-8888. That's 5-5-5-8-8-8-8."

One more thing to consider before you leave a message on a voicemail though: A recent study by Opinion Research found that cell phone users under 30 are four times more likely to respond within minutes to text messages than to voicemail. So if you know the person you are calling is young or at least very techno-friendly, it may be worth not leaving a voice message, but instead sending a text. When you do so, make sure you make the message look professional! That means no fancy shorthand like "AAMOI," "4 U," "2nite," and so on. And no smileys or fancy little symbols. Just a brief text stating why you called and why the person should call back: "Hi Pat. Tried to reach you regarding print server. Important new info. Call me. 555-8888. John."

HANDLING COMPLAINTS

Complaints are a natural part of any business and particularly so when working with active sales. Not necessarily because you are overselling but because if a person has been actively talked into buying something the decision was often taken more quickly, leaving more unanswered questions. People also feel more free to demand adaptations and tailor-made solutions than when, for example, placing an order online.

> *When people order without human interaction, for example on the Internet, they feel more responsible for their actions and for having made sure what they order exactly what suits their needs. Not because there really is any difference between saying "Yes" to a seller than clicking "Order" on a website; it is just how they view their rights and the responsibility of the contract parties.*

In my experience a good seller on a good day (when he sells a lot), tends to get fewer complaints. In a way this may seem counterintuitive; you'd think that a seller who closes many deals would have more complaints than a seller who closes just a few. However, when a good seller is having a good day, it seems his sales are straightforward, honest and completed quickly. The things that make him sell are good sales technique and plenty of self-confidence. On a bad day, a seller tends to be more desperate. He pushes the customer in the wrong way, promises too much and takes too many shortcuts. This reduces trust and lowers his sales figures and it also leads to a high complaint rate on those sales he did close.

It is important to understand that a customer's experience of the service is basically the difference between his expectations and the actual service delivered. Even if you give sell silver for half the market price, you will still receive complaints if you have told the customer that the silver will cure all sorts of illnesses and can be turned into gold by lightly tapping it against his forehead. Even if the customer got a fantastic deal he will feel upset because he didn't get what he was promised. Naturally, if you do give away silver at half the price, you wouldn't have to promise that it can magically be turned into gold; most customers would be more than happy just to get cheap silver. But sellers by nature (at least on bad days) seem to think that the more they promise the more they sell. In reality by promising more you probably lower your sales because customers suspect you are talking nonsense (and if they think one element of what you said is not true they will question the rest too) and you will spend a lot of time handling angry clients.

 So the first step of handling complaints is to remove the most fundamental reason for a customer to complain: Don't promise too much. Find the real selling points of your products and services and stick to those.

If you do have a complaint—and let's face it, it will happen— then there are some basic steps to follow.

 First of all, you need to understand why the customer is calling you and not your company's customer service line. When you are selling, you are creating trust and a personal relationship between you and the customer. If there is something wrong, if the customer has a question or a complaint two hours or two months later, chances are he will feel most comfortable calling you directly. You're the guy he knows; you're the guy who knows him and his business.

Don't get frustrated or irritated by customers calling you directly. If there is a problem with the sale, then most likely you can in fact fix it quicker than most customer support agents. Do not try to avoid answering the phone. Instead answer the call in a warm, inviting voice. Do not get upset or annoyed, even if you know there is an angry customer on the other end. At this stage you want to project confidence and control. This is important to make sure the call goes the way you want it to go.

Listen carefully to the customer's complaint. Always encourage him to explain in detail. Say things like "OK, explain exactly what the problem is and I will help you." While the customer talks, do not under any circumstances interrupt. Listen quietly until you are sure the customer is done talking. Angry or irate customers usually feel better just by having been given the chance to vent their frustration. Remember the three-second rule. Wait at least three seconds after the customer is done talking before you start talking yourself. If you interrupt the customer at this stage, even with the best of intentions, you will only increase his frustration.

Never, ever get upset yourself! Regardless of how rude the client is, getting upset will just make things worse. If this is a customer who is just frustrated, you can probably solve it by remaining cool-headed and logical. If this is one of those few percent of the population who happen to be just plain jerks, getting upset will just encourage him further. Lean back in your chair, close your eyes and think of a tropical island. It may also be a good idea to mute your microphone so that before you start talking, you actively have to unmute it. It prevents your interrupting and saying something stupid.

One in five American adults aged 18 or older, or 45.6 million people, had mental illness in 2011, according to a report from the Substance Abuse and Mental Health Services Administration. There is no reason to think 2011 was a particularly bad year. Knowing this, it simply becomes a numbers game before you will come across a real nutcase. If you close five deals per day, statistically one of your customers that day had some sort of mental disorder. Give it a year and at least one of them is going to be a complete fruitcake. Just deal with it professionally.

When the customer is done explaining, repeat a summary of the issue back to him to make sure you have understood the issue correctly.

Talk more slowly than when selling, with more deliberately worded sentences. Take longer pauses than in a sales pitch to show that you are not trying to just get rid of him, but seriously considering his complaint. Slow the whole process down.

Explain that you will make sure you come up with a solution and that you will handle the issue. Even if you can immediately identify a way of solving the problem, you should hold back a little here. It may otherwise come across as if you just want to get rid of him and make him even more suspicious.

Say that you just need to look up his case, talk to your manager or something similar and that you'll put him on hold for just a few seconds. Don't leave him there for long, just 20 to 30 seconds. Use those seconds to clear your head and formulate a reply. You want to remain apologetic and say that you take full responsibility. It is difficult to yell at or even be angry with someone who apologizes and take responsibility. *Never* try to indicate that this is the customer's own fault in one way or another! If you know how to solve the issue, come back and say something like "OK, John. Look, I fully understand your complaint, and we clearly need to take responsibility for your not being happy at this stage. What we will do for you is that we will XYZ." Note that for legal reasons it may be a bad idea to take responsibility for specific issues. But usually taking responsibility for his not being happy is sufficiently vague for it to really not mean anything. Again remember that the customer's experience of service is usually the difference between his expectations and the result. So don't promise too much.

If you need to talk to your managers, your support department or anyone else in the company before coming up with a solution, ask the customer if he prefers to wait on the line of to have you call him back. Customers tend to like the option. If the problem is complex and can be handled only by someone else in the company (IT, Legal, Finance) explain to the customer why you cannot handle the issue yourself, tell him that you will put him through to Rusty Bridges on IT, whom you know well, who will be able to assist him. Say that you will put him on hold for a short while, while you explain to Rusty what the issue is, so that the customer doesn't have to repeat everything one more time. And then make absolutely sure that you explain all the details of the case to Rusty.

If the customer is demanding a solution that is completely out of the question (and we are now probably talking about the low percentage of clients who are slightly cuckoo) you really need to make sure you don't promise too much. Lower his expectations by saying that it is impossible for your company both to refund his money and let him keep all the 500 printers for free (Such customers do exist), but that you will do your best to find a solution. Then ask him to hold while you talk to your managers.

In such cases you really need to make sure you understand the consequences of not assisting the customer in his demands. Your company may have clear policies on refunds and cancelations, but with the cuckoo clients it is often worth checking with a manager anyhow. You may not be able to give him all he is asking for, but in this day and age where a company's reputation can be ruined by one crazy guy's blog on the Internet, it may be worth making sure management is involved in the decision.

When handling someone completely off his rocker, it can help to delay the process as much as possible. You can do this by explaining that although you cannot accommodate his request, the management is meeting the second week of next month, and if he puts his complaint and demand in writing, you will present the whole case to the management to see what they can do. Hopefully by that time, the cuckoo customer will be busy pursuing some other poor seller or family member or random person on the street and may not be focusing on this case. If the customer again calls to ask for an update, you need to have lined up ideally two alternative solutions. They may not be what the customer wants, but explain that you really fought his case with the management and those two solutions are way more than the company has ever offered a customer.

For those customers who are not just crazy people complaining out of habit, but normal customers with a proper complaint, you may even find that if you handle the complaint properly it is an opportunity to sell more. Not only will it hopefully secure a long-term relationship with that customer, but the discussion regarding issues he is having may reveal that the best solution for him is to buy some other product or service you offer. If you are able to give him a really great deal, for example by packaging the product you have sold him with the product he might need even more, it can be a good opportunity for both parties. Don't fall for the temptation of unnecessary up-sale in such situations, though.

"I try not to rely on my past success alone"

HAPPY-CLAPPY STUFF

SUCCESS IS HARD WORK

As you may have gathered from the rest of this book, by nature I'm not a "happy-clappy school" sales coach. My nature is to tell people "Life is hard; deal with it through logic and hard work." A lot of other sales coaches like to focus much more on the "Think positive," "Visualize the close," "Be the customer" nonsense. Since some of them, a few, are successful in what they do too, there must be some merit to their approach.

In my opinion there is no substitute for hard sales training and extreme focus on details. My happy-clappy chapter, or motivational speech if you want to be more politically correct, will probably be much influenced by my general view on how everyone should just pull himself or herself together and work harder. There is stuff of value here even if you disagree.

A friend of mine once jokingly gave me this résumé and asked me what I thought:

> Age 22 - Failed as a business manager
> Age 23 - Ran for legislature and lost badly
> Age 24 - Started a business and went bankrupt
> Age 25 - Elected to legislature
> Age 26 - Sweetheart died
> Age 27 - Had a nervous breakdown

Age 29 - Ran for speaker and lost
Age 31 - Defeated for elector
Age 34 - Defeated for Congress
Age 37 - Elected to Congress
Age 39 - Defeated for Congress
Age 46 - Defeated to Senate
Age 47 - Defeated for Vice President
Age 49 - Defeated for Senate again
Age 51 - Elected President of the United States

It's the record of Abraham Lincoln—and the word "persistence" certainly springs to mind. It is an example often seen in inspirational books and it is not only perhaps overused, but also not entirely accurate. However, I decided to insert it here because it does illustrate well the most important features required in order to achieve success and celebrity status: desire and persistence.

No matter how talented you are, you should not expect to just walk onto the sales floor on your first day selling, put on a headset, start the autodialer and break every record in the office. As I have pointed out before (see page 39), selling is an acquired skill, just like learning math, chess or IT development. No one would ever expect, without a day of training, to sit down at a computer and write great apps. Just because practically everyone today can type on a computer doesn't mean that everyone can develop software. Selling is no different. Just because anyone can talk on the phone doesn't mean anyone can sell on the phone.

According to the US Bureau of Labor Statistics, an In-house Wholesale and Manufacturing Sales Representative makes, on average, roughly $50,000 per year. The bottom 10% earners make, on average, $35,000 per year and the 10% highest earners make, on average, $150,000 per year. A few of those made $500,000 and a small group made more than $1 million per year.

So what does this tell you about the income of sellers? Well, it tells you that it is a competitive sport. It's basically like golf: A lot of club pros make enough to get by, a selected percentage of pro players make very good money and a few top players make tons. You find this in a lot of sports, not just golf, but you also find it among, for example, doctors and lawyers. If you want to have fun with the 80-20 rule again: It is said that 20% of the top golf players in the US make 80% of the money. I am sure somewhere you'll find similar claims about top lawyers and top surgeons.

Thus when you start out as a seller you need to think like a professional. It is not enough to have watched the movie "Boiler Room" twice any more than watching an "Ally McBeal" box set on DVD is enough to become a great lawyer. You will start out at the bottom and if you want to rise in ranks and earnings you need to view yourself as a professional. You need to have the discipline and mindset of a top athlete, a professional golfer or a professional tennis player. If you wanted to become a top player in any sport you wouldn't expect to come in, play a few matches twice a week and then spend the rest of the time hanging around in bars or watching television. You need to practice, to use every available moment to become better and better. If you simply come into the office every day to do just what is required of you there and then, how can you possibly expect to reach the top? It is your responsibility to take care of your career. Don't lean back and expect your team leader, sales coach or manager to do this for you. Learning is not a passive activity.

The long and the short of it is that the sales business is one of the few industries where you can, with hard work and dedication, rise to a level of income rivaled only by top athletes. Even without a formal degree you can end up making many, many times more than well-paid CEOs or surgeons.

An extreme example is the financial services industry. Lehman Brothers, for example, back in the days when the bond trade was booming, was moving people from the mail room to the trading and sales floors. Without any training at all, people were told, "Sit here, pick up that phone, sell some bonds." Some of these people worked hard, taught themselves sales techniques and made insane amounts of money. Later companies like Lehman decided that it should try to recruit sellers with more formal education than just sorting mail and started attracting guys with MBAs from some of the most prestigious universities. Though on paper much better qualified, those would be the guys who crashed the market and caused the credit crunch and the 2008 financial crisis. Apparently you can get too smart.

Starting out as a seller, then, is basically like being given a soccer ball at the age of eight. Work hard, practice every day, treat the round object with respect and you will have a shot at success. Kick it around the backyard a few times, play a game or two a week and spend the rest of the time watching TV, and you probably won't. Treat your sales career seriously, practice every day, study sales as a science and you may have a shot at being one of those million-dollar sellers. But don't expect to become good at it just by putting on a headset at 9 AM and taking it off and heading for the bar at 6 PM.

Sales can be a wonderful career. Few people have such a direct ability to control the outcome of their careers and to influence the size of their paychecks as salespeople. (I have already pointed out in page 35 how just small changes of focus can have huge impacts on your income.) Somehow this undoubtedly positive thing has become turned into something negative by many career advisers. "A sales job is very stressful," I heard a career coach say just a few weeks back. "You are only

as good as your last month." This is something you hear a lot, even from sellers themselves. It's supposed to refer to the fact that you are always being judged on your results and as soon as one reporting period has ended the next one starts. "What a load of nonsense!" is my comment. What job with similar earning possibilities is not judged on ongoing results? In what job with such income potential will you be allowed to live on past results forever? If you're a heart surgeon and you've managed to mess up and kill your last seven patients, you can't just say, "Don't worry; my track record for 2008 and 2009 is really good." What CEO of a major company would get away by saying, "Yeah, I know we lost money for the last eight years and failed to do anything about it, but in my first five years with the company we made a nice profit"? What professional golf player would keep his status and income if he, after ten good years, suddenly started playing terribly? Everyone who is anyone, in any position of status and responsibility, is exposed to similar pressure. If you don't like it, go work for the government. As a seller, the biggest pressure to succeed should come from within yourself, your own ambitions. If you have to wait for a complaint from your manager or boss, you're already falling behind.

Top-billing salespeople are celebrated, rewarded and praised, and rightly so. They are the engines giving power to the larger machinery of their companies. But the pressure is constant, and needs to be. It will never stop—ever. Deal with it; that's what you're paid to do.

LEARN TO ALWAYS BE POSITIVE

The constant battle for success, the fight that never ends for the next sale, can be hard for every sales person. Nowhere else is this truer than for phone sales. As I have mentioned, the single most significant advantage of phone sales over face-to-face selling is the volumes of leads you can contact. This, of course, also results in a great volume of rejections. At least when cold calling, most leads are not going to have any interest either in you or your product.

No matter whether your statistics show a conversion rate of one of three, one of five or one of one hundred leads, there are going to be some days where it just feels hopeless. When you have spent the last four hours calling people who told you to take a hike in one way or another, it can be hard to convince yourself that the next call is going to be different. Yet the second you stop thinking that the next guy is definitely going to buy, you have a huge problem. Your focus is going to drop, your timing will be off, your voice will sound dull and boring. You will miss buying signals and you will push the lead in the wrong way at the wrong time. You can be pretty sure your negative thoughts are going to be self-fulfilling. As a seller, it is important to remember that you must always go into each call expecting a sale. If you feel that you don't, take a break and ask yourself why would today be any different than the day a few weeks back when you set a new team record or closed three unexpected sales in a row? You cannot influence the quality of the next leads; he may yell at you and hang up, or she may scream of joy because you called to sell her a new print just as her old printer exploded and took out two top floor windows. The only thing you as a seller can do is to do your job as well as possible. The better you do your job, the better your closing statistics are going to be. You cannot perhaps influence every single lead, but overall how you do your job directly determines your results over time. That's why every sales team has some top performers and some bottom performers. From lead to lead it may be a lottery, but over time it is about sales skills. Never forget this. Go into every call ready to fight for a sale.

IF YOU CAN'T BE, ACT

Aristotle once said, "We are what we repeatedly do; excellence is a habit." By acting like you want to become, you can make sure you slowly become what you want. Your success may influence how you behave, but how you behave may also influence your success.

Force yourself to dress and act as a successful seller, and you will normally find that it influences how you behave on the phone. Your self-confidence will increase, your sales will increase and in turn, your self-confidence will improve even more.

There are other little tricks you can use. If you want to sound positive on the phone, for example, force yourself to smile. The act of smiling influences your voice, your pace and your timing. (Try to smile and sound really angry or irritated at the same time. It's almost impossible.)

I knew a seller once who had a little makeup mirror next to his computer screen. By seeing himself he got constant feedback on how he was appearing and thus the image he was projecting both to the sales room, and through his voice, to the customers. If he was looking stressed and nervous, he knew that he was probably sounding stressed and nervous too. If he was looking irritated or angry, he knew he was probably sounding irritated or angry too. He used the mirror to spot such issues early and correct the problem before it affected his results.

SOME HAPPY-CLAPPY QUOTES

Do something positive for your career every day. It doesn't have to be something major every day—but do something! Try to improve a single sentence of your pitch, read two pages of a sales book (or just re-read two pages of this book), take an hour that would be spent watching TV to sort through your pile of old leads. But do something every day! You will be amazed how far you can get if you take small steps daily.

Remember that things are usually hard for a reason. If selling well was easy, everyone would be doing it and you would be paid peanuts.

Have fun! Super-glue the letter "R" on a colleague's keyboard (Be prepared to pay for a new one), put chili powder in a manager's coffee (Be prepared to look for a new job). Did a co-worker bring his packed suitcase to the office because he is heading straight to the airport for a weekend in Paris? Stick a small plastic bag of flour in it or replace all his belongings with wet towels (a favorite of the Salomon Brothers' trading floor). Or just do something fun in a nice way if you're so inclined. But have a little fun every day.

Don't do everything—do less better! Make sure everything you do counts. Don't read every sales book quickly—read a few good sales books well. Focus on improving one thing at a time and make sure you learn it well!

Know your own weaknesses! By knowing your own weaknesses you can spot a problem early and nip it in the bud. Whether it is a tendency to laziness, a tendency to be depressed, a problem in your sales skills—it doesn't matter. If you are aware of it, you can deal with it.

Keep track of your goals and your progress. Only if you know exactly what you want to achieve long term and short term will you ever have a chance of achieving it. Success isn't a lottery; it's hard work!

Being defeated is only a temporary condition; giving up is what makes it permanent. Even the worst sales drought is just a sales drought if you keep on fighting. Only if you give up will it become a defeat.

Every failure is a lesson in how not to do something. After enough lessons, you will know how to do it. The best way to never learn is to never try. Consider every lost sale a lesson!

Successful salespeople are just ordinary people with extraordinary determination.

Losers visualize the penalties of failure. Winners visualize the rewards of success.

Put more energy into getting started right each day than anything else. The hardest thing is always to get started, but when the morning starts well, the rest of the day will follow.

Life will throw both lead and gold at you. The trick is to know when to catch and when to duck.

And finally, remember that today is gone tomorrow. Tomorrow may be another day, but you will never get another shot at today. Margaret Thatcher once said, "Look at a day when you are supremely satisfied at the end. It's not a day when you lounge around doing nothing; it's when you've had everything to do, and you've done." So make sure you make today count!

INDEX

DID YOU LIKE THIS BOOK?

Find more similar books on
http://acanexus-publishing.com.